Discoverers and Inventors
READER'S THEATER
DEVELOP READING FLUENCY AND TEXT COMPREHENSION SKILLS

Written by
Pamela Jennett

Editor: Alaska Hults

Illustrator: Corbin Hillam

Cover Illustrator: Amy Vangsgard

Designer: Jane Wong-Saunders

Cover Designer: Barbara Peterson

Art Director: Tom Cochrane

Project Director: Carolea Williams

Table of Contents

6 = total number of parts

INTRODUCTION

Fluency instruction provides a bridge between being able to "read" a text and being able to understand it. Readers who decode word by word sound plodding and choppy. They are too busy figuring out the words to think about what they are reading. Fluent readers are accurate, quick, and able to read with expression. They make the reading sound interesting. Beyond the experience of the listener, fluent readers are also demonstrating skills that are crucial to their understanding of what they read. Fluent readers recognize words at a glance, group words into meaningful phrases, and move beyond the struggle to decode individual words. They are able to focus on making sense of what they read.

Reader's Theater is an exciting way to help students improve reading fluency without being too time intensive for the teacher. It requires no props and no additional teaching skills on your part, and it is not difficult to manage. Reader's Theater promotes better reading comprehension because students who have learned to read a passage expressively also come to better understand its meaning. In addition, research says that these gains transfer well to new text. Reader's Theater also addresses standards in listening while providing a fun environment for everyone involved. When students practice their lines, they read and reread the same passages. Under your direction, they gradually add more expression, read more smoothly, and find any subtle meanings in the passages.

The scripts in *Discoverers and Inventors Reader's Theater* are intended to be read in large groups of 7 to 11 students. Each script is prefaced by an activity that focuses on vocabulary from the script, the factual and fictional background of the piece, fluency instruction specific to that script, and comprehension questions that span the levels of Bloom's Taxonomy. Each script is followed by activities related to the content of the script.

These scripts are designed for fluency instruction. While they are based on factual information about the time period or characters, many of the characters and scenes are entirely fictional. The overall purpose is to provide students with text at their reading level that is fun to read. The background section that precedes each script provides additional information about the characters or the period around which the script is built. All the scripts provide the following hallmarks of a good Reader's Theater text:

• fast-moving dialogue
• action
• humor
• narrative parts

Discoverers and Inventors Reader's Theater provides hours of fluency practice that features characters students know and may even admire. The large-group format gives students an opportunity to work together to craft an entertaining reading for a peer or adult audience.

How To Use This Book

Each Reader's Theater script should be covered over the course of five practice days (although those days do not need to be consecutive). The first day should include some or all of the elements of the suggested reading instruction. It should also include an expressive reading by you of the script as students read along silently. On each of the following days, give students an opportunity to practice their reading. On the final day, have each group read its script for the class.

Five sections that support reading instruction precede each script. You will find **vocabulary, background information** for the script, **a brief description of each character,** specific **coaching for fluency instruction,** and **comprehension questions** that progress from the simplest level of understanding to the most complex.

On the first day of instruction, briefly discuss with students the vocabulary. Each vocabulary list includes a short activity to help students understand the meaning of each vocabulary word. For example, the vocabulary activity for Archimedes (page 7) asks students to create a chart that clarifies the meaning of one of the words.

Next, use the background and information about each character to tell students what the script will be about and describe the characters.

Read aloud the script, modeling clear enunciation and a storyteller's voice. Do not be afraid to exaggerate your expression—it will hold the attention of your audience and stick more firmly in their minds when they attempt to mimic you later. Model the pacing you expect from them as they read.

Finish the reading instruction by discussing the fluency tips with students and having them answer the questions in the comprehension section.

Now it is time to give students a copy of the script! Use the following schedule of student practice for a five-day instruction period.

Day 1	After following the steps outlined on page 4, give each student a personal copy of the script. Pair students and have Partner A read all the parts on the first page, Partner B read all the parts on the second page, and so on.
Days 2 and 3	Assign students to a group. Give each group a script for each student, and have each student highlight a different part. Have students gather to read aloud the script as many times as time permits. Have them change roles with each reading by exchanging the highlighted scripts. Move from group to group, providing feedback and additional modeling as needed. At the *end* of day 3, assign roles or have students agree on a role to own.

Day 4	Have each group read aloud the script. Move from group to group and provide feedback. Have students discuss their favorite lines at the end of each reading and why the manner in which they are read works well. Repeat.
Day 5	Have each group perform its script for the rest of the class (or other audience members provided by buddy classes and/or school personnel).

Throughout the week, or as time permits, provide students with the activities that follow each script. These are optional and do not have to be completed to provide fluency instruction; however, many provide students with additional background information that may help them better understand the characters or setting of the script.

Additional Tips

- Use the Reader's Theater Planning reproducible (page 6) to track the assigned roles for each group and to jot down any informal observations you make for assessment. Use these observations to drive future fluency instruction.

- Notice that there are no staging directions in the scripts. These plays are written to be read expressively in a storyteller's voice. If the focus is placed on *acting out* the script, students will shift their focus from the reading to the movement. If students become enchanted with a script and want to act it out, invite them to do so after they have mastered the reading. Then, have the group go through the script and brainstorm their own staging directions to jot in the margins.

- To fit fluency instruction into an already full day of instruction, it will work best to have all groups work on the same script. This will permit you to complete the first day's activities as a whole class. Students will enjoy hearing how another child reads the same lines, and some mild competition to read expressively will only foster additional effort.

- If you have too many roles for the number of students in a group, assign one child more than one part.

- If you have too many students for parts, divide up the narrator parts. As a rule, these parts tend to have longer lines.

- The roles with the greatest and least number of words to read are noted in the teacher pages. The ⬆ and ⬇ indicate a higher or lower *word count*. They are not a reflection of reading level. The narrator parts usually reflect the highest reading level. However, less fluent readers may benefit from having fewer words to master. More advanced readers may benefit from the challenge of the greater word count.

Reader's Theater Planning

Group 1   Script: _____

Name	Part	Notes:

Group 2   Script: _____

Name	Part	Notes:

Group 3   Script: _____

Name	Part	Notes:

Discoverers and Inventors Reader's Theater © 2004 Creative Teaching Press

ARCHIMEDES (287–212 B.C.)

DISCOVERERS AND INVENTORS

VOCABULARY

Discuss each of the following words with students. Then, have students choose one of the words to research in a print or an online encyclopedia or dictionary. Have students create a chart that teaches the class more about their word.

buoyancy: the upward force that a fluid exerts on an object less dense than itself

Eureka: a Greek word meaning "I have found it!"

sire: a title of respect for a king or monarch

stench: an unpleasant smell

BACKGROUND

Archimedes did indeed discover the principle of buoyancy, and he did discover it as a result of the king's suspicions about his crown. However, the story of his naked leap from his bath and his run through the streets is a legend—we do not know how much or little of it is true. The characters of Archimedes, Pheidias, and King Hiero are real; the others, and the events of this script, were created to add interest to this story.

PARTS

- Narrator 1
- Narrator 2

Archimedes (AR kuh MEE deez): a 30-year-old inventor and mathematician

King Hiero (HIGH uh row): King of Syracuse on the island of Sicily

Desma (DEZ muh): Archimedes' 48-year-old mother

Queen Anassa (uh NASS uh): wife of King Hiero

Heracleides (her uh klee AY deez): a friendly neighbor

*Pheidias (FAY DEE uhz): Archimedes' 50-year-old father, an astronomer

Hypus (HIGH puhs): a 20-year-old assistant to the king

*Apelles (uh PEL us): a craftsman

- Old Woman: a friend and neighbor of Archimedes

- Young Woman: a friend and neighbor of Archimedes

*May be read by the same student

FLUENCY INSTRUCTION

Have students discuss the ages of the characters to help them reflect the maturity level in their reading. When you read aloud the script for students, have them listen for the following:

- When the king becomes suspicious of the crown, it is reflected in his voice and his manner. Discuss how he tries to hide his suspicions from the others.

- When a character is in deep thought or distracted, his or her speech is halting and soft. Have students point out places in the script where a character is distracted.

- Ask students to demonstrate how people talk when they mutter. Explain that people mutter when they think out loud, aren't sure of what they are saying, or if they don't want someone else to hear what they are saying. Have students find the place in the script where a character mutters the lines. Ask students to determine why the character is muttering at this point.

COMPREHENSION

After you read aloud the script, ask students these questions:

1. Who is Desma? What role does she play in the story?

2. Why would Archimedes' behavior lead people to conclude he is crazy?

3. Which character would you choose to be in this story? Why?

4. Tell about a time you have been suspicious about someone's behavior or actions.

5. What do you think will happen to the craftsman? Why?

THE TRUTH IS REVEALED

Discoverers and Inventors Reader's Theater © 2004 Creative Teaching Press

PARTS

Narrator 1
Narrator 2
Archimedes (AR kuh MEE deez):
 a 30-year-old inventor and mathematician
King Hiero (HIGH uh row): King of Syracuse
 on the island of Sicily
Desma (DEZ muh): Archimedes' 48-year-old
 mother
Queen Anassa (uh NASS uh): wife of
 King Hiero
Heracleides (her uh klee AY deez):
 a friendly neighbor
Pheidias (FAY DEE uhz): Archimedes'
 50-year-old father, an astronomer
Hypus (HIGH puhs): a 20-year-old assistant to
 the king
Apelles (uh PEL us): a craftsman
Old Woman: a friend and neighbor
 of Archimedes
Young Woman: a friend and neighbor
 of Archimedes

Narrator 1: We find ourselves on the island of Sicily in the city of Syracuse. The king and queen give audience to a craftsman.

Narrator 2: The king hired the craftsman to make him a new crown. The king gave the craftsman some gold from which to make the crown.

Narrator 1: Now the crown is finished. The craftsman has returned to the king's court to present the new crown.

Hypus: Your highness, may I present the craftsman Apelles.

King Hiero: Come forward, Apelles. I want to see the crown you have made me.

Apelles: Sire, I have used all of my skills to make this beautiful crown for you. There is no other like it in all of Greece.

Narrator 2: The room is silent as everyone watches Apelles unfold a cloth to reveal the crown.

Queen Anassa: Ohhh, it is wonderful! It is truly a crown for your royal head, my king.

King Hiero: [grinning] Indeed. I am very pleased. Hypus, take the crown and place it in my hands. I wish to see this crown more closely.

Hypus: As you wish, sire.

Narrator 1: Apelles hands the crown to Hypus. He places the crown carefully in King Hiero's hands.

Narrator 2: But as he does so, the king's smile changes to a frown. He looks puzzled.

Queen Anassa: What is it?

THE TRUTH IS REVEALED

Hypus: Sire, have I made you angry somehow?

King Hiero: [muttering] It is nothing. [to the craftsman] Apelles, you may go. If I need you again, I know where to find you.

Narrator 1: Apelles bows to the king and queen. As he walks away, a smile appears on his face. His smile grows wider as he leaves the room.

Narrator 2: The king grows more and more unhappy. He orders Hypus to leave the room.

Queen Anassa: What is the matter? Do you not like this new crown?

King Hiero: It is not the design I am unhappy with.

Queen: Then what is it?

King Hiero: Something is not right. The crown is heavy, like it is made of solid gold, but it is too big. I think this craftsman has cheated me.

Queen Anassa: How can that be? It looks like gold to me.

King Hiero: It is gold on the outside. But I suspect Apelles has used silver on the inside and covered it with gold. He has kept the rest of the gold for himself.

Queen Anassa: How can you prove it?

King Hiero: Pheidias has a son who is very smart. He does experiments all the time. I think he will be able to give me an answer.

Narrator 1: King Hiero sends a messenger to the house of Pheidias. The messenger explains to Pheidias and Desma that their son is needed by the king.

Narrator 2: Pheidias and Desma do not know where their son is, but they assure the messenger that Archimedes will be happy to help the king.

Desma: Once again, there is important work for Archimedes and he is nowhere to be found.

Pheidias: Not to worry, wife. He will be back soon. I ordered the servants to take him to the baths. He has been so busy with his experiments, I do not believe he has bathed in days.

Desma: I wondered why the air was fresher today. I thought perhaps the stables had been cleared.

Narrator 1: Later, Archimedes learns from his mother and father that he is wanted by the king.

Discoverers and Inventors Reader's Theater © 2004 Creative Teaching Press

THE TRUTH IS REVEALED

Narrator 2: Archimedes goes to King Hiero, looking and smelling cleaner than he has been in days. The king could not have called for him at a better time.

King Hiero: Ah, Archimedes. You have a brilliant mind. I need your help. I suspect I am being tricked. Is this crown pure gold? Or is it silver covered in gold? I cannot tell. Maybe it is all in my head.

Queen Anassa: I believe it is on your head, sire.

Archimedes: [holding the crown] It does look like gold. But shouldn't a crown of this size be much heavier? Something does not look right.

King Hiero: I knew it was not all on my head, er, in my head. That is the problem. Now, Archimedes, can you find the answer?

Archimedes: My king, nothing makes me happier than finding the answers to problems.

Narrator 1: Archimedes begins to think about the crown. He knows that gold is very heavy.

Narrator 2: He also knows that the same amount of silver is not as heavy as gold. How can he prove which metal is in the crown?

Narrator 1: For days, Archimedes thinks about the problem. He is so obsessed that he barely eats or speaks, and he certainly does not bathe!

Young Woman: Desma, is your son working on another problem?

Desma: Why, yes, he is. Have you heard about it?

Old Woman: No, it was the stench in the air. We knew that once again Archimedes must be hard at work.

Young Woman: You must find your son a wife. He needs someone to keep him fed and clean.

Desma: Are either of you volunteering for the job?

Old Woman: Oh no. It is too much work for me.

Desma: And now you know why he is not married.

Narrator 1: Finally, Archimedes' neighbors can take no more. They ask his friend Heracleides to help.

Narrator 2: Heracleides takes Archimedes to the public baths. Archimedes is so deep in thought, he pays little attention to his friend or to his bath.

Archimedes: Don't you think you have filled my bath a bit full, Heracleides?

Heracleides: Yes, but I think the more water the better. I would not be surprised if I had to refill the bath with fresh water more than once. How can you live with yourself?

Archimedes: What? Oh, yes, thanks. I can manage.

Narrator 1: Archimedes steps into the bath. As he sits down in the water, the water sloshes over the sides of the tub.

Narrator 2: The sloshing water catches Archimedes' attention. Suddenly, his eyes open wide and he yells …

Archimedes: [loudly] Eureka! Eureka!

Heracleides: What is it? Is the water too hot?

Narrator 1: Archimedes ignores his friend. He jumps out of the water.

Narrator 2: He also ignores his clothes. He runs outside naked, yelling …

Archimedes: [loudly] Eureka! I have the answer at last!

Heracleides: What? That you have lost your mind? People are staring, Archimedes. You have no clothes. No one will listen to your answers if they think you are crazy.

Narrator 1: Archimedes is too excited to be stopped. He runs through the streets without a stitch of clothing.

Narrator 2: He flings open the door to his home.

Desma: Ahhh! My son has lost his mind!

Pheidias: Here is a towel, Archimedes. Cover yourself. What has possessed you to act this way?

Archimedes: Tell King Hiero I will see him now. I have his answer at last.

Narrator 1: Later that day, Archimedes stands before the king, properly dressed of course. He has asked the king for the crown, the same amount of pure gold, the same amount of silver, and three vessels of water.

King Hiero: I hear that you have been scaring the citizens of our city, Archimedes.

Archimedes: I am sorry, King Hiero. But I was so excited I forgot myself.

King Hiero: I do not think others will forget you for quite some time.

Discoverers and Inventors Reader's Theater © 2004 Creative Teaching Press

THE TRUTH IS REVEALED

Archimedes: When I sat in my bath, my body displaced the water. The water sloshed over the sides of the tub. When I stepped out of the bath, the tub was not so full anymore.

King Hiero: What does that have to do with my crown?

Archimedes: Everything! Watch.

Narrator 2: Archimedes marks the side of a vessel of water to show the water level. Then, he places the king's crown into the vessel. The water level goes up. He marks this new water level.

Archimedes: See how the water level goes up? The more dense an object is, the more water it displaces. Silver is not as dense as gold. So the amount of silver that weighs the same as this amount of gold displaces more water because the gold is more dense.

Narrator 1: King Hiero stares as Archimedes places the silver in another vessel. The water level is higher than the first vessel with the crown. Then, Archimedes places the pure gold in the third vessel. The water level does not rise as high as the water with the crown.

King Hiero: If my new crown was made of pure gold, the water level of the vessels with my crown and the pure gold should be the same. But the water level of the vessel with my crown is between the gold and the silver.

Archimedes: Yes, sire, your crown is made of gold *and* silver.

King Hiero: Bring me that craftsman. He has some explaining to do. Archimedes, where are you going? Archimedes?

Narrator 2: Archimedes is already deep in thought. He has discovered the principle of buoyancy. Archimedes realizes he has other experiments to do. And he is clean again for two more weeks, at least!

Discoverers and Inventors Reader's Theater © 2004 Creative Teaching Press

RELATED LESSONS

Displacement and Buoyancy

OBJECTIVE
Investigate the effects of buoyancy on various objects.

ACTIVITY
Explain that buoyancy is how things float. Buoyancy can refer to something floating in a liquid, such as water, or a gas, such as the air. Boats and balloons have buoyancy. In order for an object to have buoyancy, it must be less dense than the liquid or gas it is floating in. Divide the class into small groups Give each group **a clear container of water**, a **grease pencil**, and **several objects of various materials, shapes, and sizes.** Have students place each object in the container of water and determine if it is buoyant. For those objects that are buoyant, ask students to mark the water level before and after the object is placed in the container. Have students determine which floating objects cause a greater change in the water level.

The Greek Alphabet

OBJECTIVE
Read and answer questions about the ancient Greek alphabet.

ACTIVITY
Give each student **The Greek Alphabet reproducible (page 15).** Explain that the Greeks established an alphabet that included the vowel sounds, an improvement over a previous alphabet developed by other cultures in the region. Explain that the ancient Greek alphabet has some letters that are not on the chart and not all English letters have a single Greek equivalent. Have students identify the letters that most closely resemble those in English. Point out the English words at the bottom of the page that have Greek origins. Ask students to think of another word that has the same Greek root word to add to the list.

ANSWERS
1. horse
2. captain
3. mother
4. ϚΟϞ
5. ΑϞϿϞϟϞΑϞ
6. ϚϞϞϿϞϟϿϿ
7. *Possible answers: pentagram, pentathlon*
8. *Possible answers: biography, biomass*
9. *Possible answers: automatic, autograph, autobiography*
10. *Possible answers: geode, geography, geometry*

Name_____ Date _____

The Greek Alphabet

Directions: Use the Greek letters below to decode the words.

Greek Letter	Greek Name of Letter	English Letter	Greek Letter	Greek Name of Letter	English Letter
 A	alpha	A		lambda	L
 B	beta	B		mu	M
	gamma	C	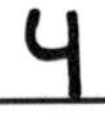	nu	N
 △	delta	D	O	omicron	O
	epsilon	E		pi	P
	digamma	F	 φ	koppa	Q
	heta	H		rho	R
	iota	I		sigma	S
 K	kappa	K	 T	tau	T

1.  ᘰO4Sᗺ _____

2.  ᒾAᒾTAᔆ५ _____

3.  ५OTᘰᗺᖴ _____

Use the Greek letters to write these words.

4. son

[   ]

5. American

[   ]

6. science

[   ]

Many English words come from Greek words. The Greek root and one English word is shown below. Write another word that uses the same root.

7. penta (five)
pentagon
_____

8. bio (life)
biology
_____

9. auto (self)
automobile
_____

10. geo (earth)
geocentric
_____

Discoverers and Inventors Reader's Theater © 2004 Creative Teaching Press

HYPATIA
(355–415)

DISCOVERERS AND INVENTORS

VOCABULARY

Discuss each of the following words with students. Then, have volunteers use each word in a sentence to demonstrate its meaning.

dejected: low in spirits; depressed

gory: covered with blood

lopsided: heavier or larger on one side than the other

precarious: not stable; easily tipped over or lacking in security

tunic: a long, loose top worn cinched with a belt

BACKGROUND

Hypatia of Alexandria is one of the first known women to study science and mathematics. Her father strived to make her the "perfect human" by educating her in many different fields. She was a respected teacher and earned the respect of other scholars of her time. Little is recorded about her mother, and it is not known if she had any siblings.

PARTS

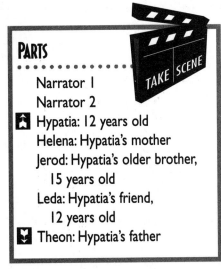

Narrator 1
Narrator 2
Hypatia: 12 years old
Helena: Hypatia's mother
Jerod: Hypatia's older brother,
    15 years old
Leda: Hypatia's friend,
    12 years old
Theon: Hypatia's father

FLUENCY INSTRUCTION

Have students discuss the ages of the characters to help them reflect the maturity level in their reading. When you read aloud the script for students, have them listen for the following:

- On occasion, one narrator begins and the other ends the same sentence. Have students identify where an ellipsis indicates that one narrator begins the line and the other ends it. Ask volunteers to practice reading these lines to show how it should sound as though one character is finishing the line of another.

- Hypatia's parents are older than the children in the play, but their ages are not given. Have students estimate the ages of the parents and demonstrate how the voice of Helena would be different than the voice of Hypatia.

- Jerod often speaks with sarcasm. Discuss with students what it means to be sarcastic (using wit to be ironic or to poke fun at another). Have them identify other places where the characters use sarcasm in their speech.

- Commas signal a pause. Reread the line *Helena: Yes, I have to admit.* Have students read this line pausing at the comma and without pausing. Ask them to explain how the comma helps the meaning of the sentence. Then, have students continue reading the rest of Helena's lines and focus on the commas in the last sentence.

COMPREHENSION

After you read aloud the script, ask students these questions:

1. Why does Leda call Hypatia "scholar-girl"?

2. Summarize what happens in the story.

3. Who seems to be more comfortable in the kitchen, Jerod or Hypatia? Why do you think this is?

4. Which of the characters do you think you are most like? Why?

5. If you could talk to Leda, what would you say to convince her of the importance of a good education?

A Family Day in the Kitchen

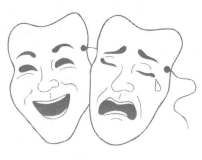

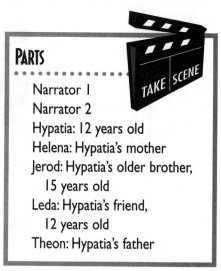

Parts

Narrator 1
Narrator 2
Hypatia: 12 years old
Helena: Hypatia's mother
Jerod: Hypatia's older brother,
   15 years old
Leda: Hypatia's friend,
   12 years old
Theon: Hypatia's father

Narrator 1: It is morning in Alexandria. The sun shines brightly. Already, at 10:00, the cobbled stones of the street are warm from the heat of the sun.

Narrator 2: Hypatia sits on the stone stoop outside her front door. She intently studies the paper in her lap.

Narrator 1: Hypatia is so absorbed in her studies that she does not hear her friend approach.

Leda: Hey, scholar-girl!

Hypatia: [startled] Ahh! You frightened me! Leda, you shouldn't sneak up on people like that. And stop calling me that.

Leda: I think it is a pretty fitting name. And how can I not sneak up on you? When you are into your studies, it is as though you are deaf, dumb, and blind to any other living thing. That's why I call you that.

Hypatia: You are out and about early today.

Leda: What do you have planned? As if I didn't know. Let's go have some fun. You can't stay here reading all day.

Hypatia: But I like to read! And write. If you learned how, you'd enjoy it too. I could teach you, you know.

Leda: Nice try, but my mother frowns on that. She says I must prepare myself to take care of my own household someday. That's okay with me. If I learned to read, I'd probably bury my nose in books all the time, like you do.

Jerod: That's why Hypatia reads you know. That way she can get out of doing other things.

Leda: Oh, hello, Jerod. What's wrong with your sister? You aren't such a bookworm. How did she become one?

Jerod: Oh, I spend plenty of time reading too. Father makes sure of that, but it is expected of me. Father just thinks it's important for us to be well-read. Hypatia just takes that idea to the extreme.

A Family Day in the Kitchen

Hypatia: Anyway, I don't even get to do what I want. My mother, like your mother, has ideas on how I should spend my time. And today she won out over my father.

Helena: Hypatia! Oh, there you are. I thought you understood you were to help me today. Good morning, Leda.

Leda: Good morning, ma'am.

Hypatia: I know, Mother. I was getting a bit of studying in before we began.

Helena: Studying! You are always studying. I told your father that no good would come of all this learning. However, he is your father and he insists you be educated.

Leda: I think my father would be happy if his sons studied as hard as Hypatia.

Helena: Yes, I have to admit that. She knows just as much as her brother and much more than many other young men, older or younger. Come, Hypatia, I want you to help me make the loaves of bread.

Leda: Really? Oh, I'd love to see that!

Hypatia: Never mind, Leda. I think you said you were off to do something fun?

Jerod: [smiling] Don't worry, Leda. I'll be there to see it all. I'll be sure and give you all the gory details later.

Narrator 1: Dejected, Hypatia follows her mother into the kitchen. Her mother has already set supplies for breadmaking out on the tabletop.

Narrator 2: Jerod proceeds to stoke the fire in the wood oven. Hypatia sets her books on the edge of the table, a little closer than she should.

Narrator 1: A bowl of flour is perched in a precarious manner as Hypatia grabs at it, barely preventing a disaster. She manages to get flour all over her hands and lower arms.

Jerod: Whoa, nice catch, sis! Mother, look. She's already floured her hands to knead the bread.

Helena: Please be careful, Hypatia. That is the last of the flour. I don't want to have to go to the market today to get more.

Hypatia: I'll go for you. I don't mind!

Helena: Nice try, but you won't get out of here that easily.

Jerod: I don't know. This could be dangerous. Hypatia in the kitchen? It's a pretty scary thought, if you ask me.

Discoverers and Inventors Reader's Theater © 2004 Creative Teaching Press

A FAMILY DAY IN THE KITCHEN

Hypatia: No one did ask you, so please be quiet.

Helena: Here, Hypatia. Stir this into the flour. Mix it only until it makes a sticky dough. Let me know when it gets that way.

Hypatia: See, Jerod. I can handle this. This isn't so tough.

Narrator 1: As Hypatia stirs the dough, the sticky stuff gets on her hands. She tries to wipe it off on her tunic, but it just makes a mess.

Helena: Oh my goodness, Hypatia, what are you doing?

Jerod: You have dough in your hair! Does this mean we're going to have hair in our dough?

Hypatia: My hair was in my eyes. I tried to push it out of the way, but this stupid dough sticks to everything. I wonder if there is a way to make dough less sticky?

Jerod: [sighing] You can look it up in a book later. Here, I'll finish the mixing. Go wash your hands at the water basin.

Narrator 2: Hypatia leaves the room. Jerod continues to stir the dough.

Jerod: This is a bad idea, Mother. We may be going without bread for dinner this evening.

Helena: That's enough, Jerod. If you can't be a help, then go elsewhere. You aren't doing anyone any good if you are making a pest of yourself at Hypatia's expense.

Hypatia: Okay, I'm back and ready to start again. You know, I wonder if it would make a difference if we added some more oil to the bread?

Helena: No, it won't rise properly with too much oil. Here, sprinkle this flour over the dough as Jerod continues to mix it. Continue adding flour until it becomes stiff and spongy.

Jerod: [whispering to Hypatia] Think of it as a simple experiment, sister. [loudly] Hey! The flour goes on the dough, not on my arms!

Hypatia: [sarcastically] Oops! [thoughtfully] Actually, maybe you're right! We could try loaves with different amounts of flour and oil and—

Helena: Not today, thank you. This is our dinner bread and we will not experiment with it. Now, Jerod, divide the dough in half. Each of you can help knead a loaf.

Hypatia: Is there a science to this?

Jerod: I don't know about that, but it's easy enough. Use the heel of your hands and push the dough away from you. Fold the dough over and do it again. Good!

Discoverers and Inventors Reader's Theater © 2004 Creative Teaching Press

A Family Day in the Kitchen

Hypatia: This isn't so bad, and it's not so sticky any more. Hey! The property of the dough is changing! It's becoming spongy, almost bouncy!

Theon: A family day in the kitchen, I see.

Hypatia: Hello, Father. I'm making bread. Not only can I do algebra, and track the path of the stars, I can make my own dinner, too!

Helena: Let's finish the bread first. Then, we'll declare a victory. Dinner remains to be seen.

Theon: From the way Hypatia is kneading that bread, I'll guess it will be dead by dinner.

Helena: Hypatia! Not so hard! You don't have to kill it!

Hypatia: Oh! Sorry, I got a little carried away.

Helena: Now shape the dough into a loaf and set it on the wooden paddle. Then, make three shallow slashes in the top with the knife.

Narrator 1: Jerod does as he is told and slides a perfect-looking loaf into the oven. He hands the paddle to Hypatia.

Narrator 2: Hypatia shapes her dough into an odd, lopsided loaf. She makes slices in the top.

Hypatia: [to herself] Oh, I should have put it on the paddle first.

Narrator 1: She sets the paddle next to the dough and tries to pull the dough onto the paddle. When that does not work, she lifts the dough up to set it on the paddle . . .

Narrator 2: . . . and half of it falls on the floor. Hypatia looks around and realizes that no one is watching her.

Hypatia: Hmmm, it looks somehow deflated. I suppose it will puff up again in the oven. No one will ever know.

Narrator 1: Later, Helena pulls the loaves of bread from the oven.

Jerod: What is that thing?

Hypatia: Is that my loaf of bread? What happened?

Narrator 2: Instead of a nice rounded loaf of bread, Hypatia's loaf is no thicker than a board. While Jerod's loaf is a toasty brown, Hypatia has flecks of black peppering on the side of her loaf.

Theon: Did I ever tell you what an excellent mathematician you are, Hypatia?

Hypatia: Oh, Father. You don't have to humor me. I can tell I need to learn a lot more before I'll master the science of cooking.

Discoverers and Inventors Reader's Theater © 2004 Creative Teaching Press

RELATED LESSONS

Seven Wonders of the World

OBJECTIVE

Research and report on the Seven Wonders of the Ancient World.

ACTIVITY

Explain that Hypatia lived in the city of Alexandria. Alexandria was the site of one of the Seven Wonders of the Ancient World, the Pharos of Alexandria. The Pharos was the forerunner of all lighthouses. Provide students with **research materials and/or the Internet.** Ask them to research each of the Seven Wonders of the Ancient World. Have students present to the class the name of their wonder, the location where it was found, its purpose, and the civilization that built it.

Alexandria

OBJECTIVE

Read and answer questions about the city of Alexandria.

ACTIVITY

Give each student the **Alexandria** and **Ancient City reproducibles (pages 23–24).** Explain that students will read about the ancient city of Alexandria and its importance in history. Have students read the passage and answer the questions. Ask them to share their answers with the class.

ANSWERS

1. Alexander the Great established the city of Alexandria in 331 B.C.
2. Alexandria had an important location at the center of the routes that led to Asia, Africa, and Europe. It was also a center for learning.
3. Alexandria was in a good location. Lots of people came from all over the world to visit and stay.
4. *Possible answer:* If people came to Alexandria for the learning, maybe they would stay and help make it a better place to live.
5. *Possible answer:* Hypatia might have enjoyed the museum, where she could discuss her ideas with others.
6. *Answers will vary.*

Alexandria

Alexandria was a city in ancient Egypt. It was named after Alexander the Great, who conquered Egypt and established the city in 331 B.C. Alexandria was one of the largest and most important cities of this time. One of the reasons for this was its location. Alexandria was located at the center of the main routes that led to Asia, Africa, and Europe. Alexandria was located on the Nile delta and had a harbor large enough to accommodate many warships and trading vessels. Many goods were brought into and traded in Alexandria. Its prosperity attracted many people and, in turn, it also became a center for learning during the Greek and Roman civilizations.

Ptolemy ruled Alexandria after the death of Alexander the Great. He made it the capital city of Egypt and it remained the capital for almost 300 years. It was during Ptolemy's rule that many temples, buildings, museums, and libraries were built. Two of its famous structures were the great Museum and the Library of Alexandria.

The Museum of Alexandria was not like the museums we have today. Instead, it was a place of learning and study. Open courtyards and tree-lined gardens encouraged people to come together and present their ideas to one another. Scholars debated ideas and philosophies. The museum came to represent the best of Greek learning at the time.

The Library of Alexandria became a center of Greek culture. The library held as many as a half a million volumes and was the largest collection of books in the world at that time. The works of many famous Greek writers, philosophers, and scientists could be found in the vast collection of books. Some of these individuals also served as librarians and helped others with their studies and research. Unfortunately, in 48 B.C., a battle was fought between the Egyptians and the Romans. A fire was ignited during the fighting and the library was destroyed. The great collection of Greek knowledge housed within the library was lost for all time.

Ancient City

1. Who was the founder of Alexandria and when was it established?

2. Give two reasons why Alexandria became an important city.

3. Alexandria became a prosperous city. *Prosperous* means *marked with wealth or success*. What was it about Alexandria that led it to become so prosperous?

4. Why do you think the rulers of Alexandria encouraged learning and the exchange of new ideas?

5. Of the places mentioned in the passage, where do you think Hypatia would have spent her time? Why?

6. If these places existed today, would you prefer to study at the Museum or the Library of Alexandria? What are the reasons for your choice?

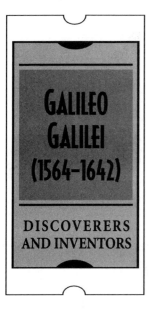

GALILEO
GALILEI
(1564–1642)

DISCOVERERS
AND INVENTORS

VOCABULARY

Discuss each of the following words with students. Then, have students find each word in the dictionary, copy the definition, and write the guide words from the dictionary page for that word.

arc: the curved path of a swinging object

gravity: a natural force that draws objects toward the center of the earth

heresy: an opinion or belief that goes against accepted religious beliefs

pendulum: a weight hung on a string so that it can swing back and forth

telescope: a device used to make distant objects appear closer

BACKGROUND

Galileo Galilei was always a curious child and grew up to be a curious man. While his father wanted him to be a doctor, Galileo was most happy experimenting with things he observed around him. He realized early on that many of the accepted teachings of science could not be proved by the scientific process. He set out to use the scientific process to either prove or disprove theories of science. Many of his findings went against the beliefs that were accepted by the religious authorities of the day.

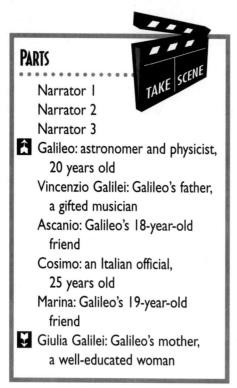

PARTS

Narrator 1
Narrator 2
Narrator 3
Galileo: astronomer and physicist, 20 years old
Vincenzio Galilei: Galileo's father, a gifted musician
Ascanio: Galileo's 18-year-old friend
Cosimo: an Italian official, 25 years old
Marina: Galileo's 19-year-old friend
Giulia Galilei: Galileo's mother, a well-educated woman

FLUENCY INSTRUCTION

Have students discuss the ages of the characters to help them reflect the maturity level in their reading. When you read aloud the script for students, have them listen for the following:

- None of the characters are children. Their speech is slower and more sophisticated than a child may speak. Have students pay attention to how the young adults speak to each other and how that would be different than the way they speak to older adults and authority figures.

- Galileo's father thinks that Galileo wastes his time and needs to get a real job. His frustration becomes apparent in his voice when he speaks with a higher pitch and in a louder tone. Have students identify at least two places in the script where Vincenzio is frustrated by his son's behavior.

- Your voice rises very steeply at the end of a question that is both an exclamation and a question such as Galileo's confused *What?! Are you crazy?!*

- Italics are used to show where a word should be stressed to add meaning to the sentence such as on the line **Ascanio:** Now *that* would have made sense.

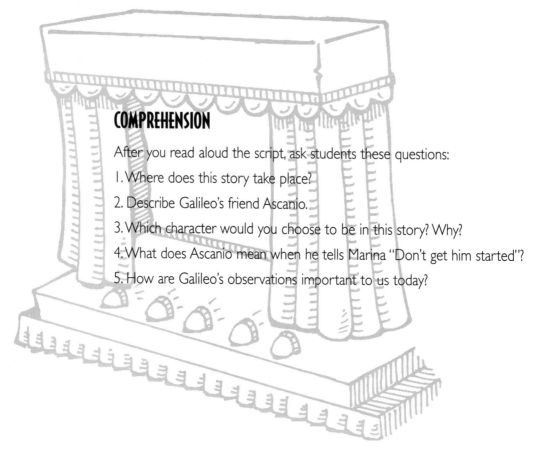

COMPREHENSION

After you read aloud the script, ask students these questions:

1. Where does this story take place?

2. Describe Galileo's friend Ascanio.

3. Which character would you choose to be in this story? Why?

4. What does Ascanio mean when he tells Marina "Don't get him started"?

5. How are Galileo's observations important to us today?

THINGS ARE LOOKING UP!

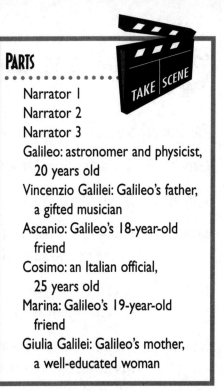

PARTS

Narrator 1
Narrator 2
Narrator 3
Galileo: astronomer and physicist, 20 years old
Vincenzio Galilei: Galileo's father, a gifted musician
Ascanio: Galileo's 18-year-old friend
Cosimo: an Italian official, 25 years old
Marina: Galileo's 19-year-old friend
Giulia Galilei: Galileo's mother, a well-educated woman

Narrator 1: Galileo Galilei was born in 1564. He was the oldest of seven children.

Narrator 2: His family lived in the city of Pisa, a small town in Italy. Yes, this is the same place with the famous leaning tower.

Narrator 3: When you are the oldest of seven children, you don't want to spend a lot of time hanging around the house. And neither did Galileo.

Narrator 1: Galileo was a curious young man and he spent a lot of time observing the world around him. He wondered how things worked and why things happened.

Narrator 2: He spent so much time wondering about things that his parents became a little worried.

Vincenzio: Giulia, have you seen Galileo? I can't seem to find him anywhere.

Giulia: No, I haven't.

Vincenzio: It's eight o'clock at night. Where could he be?

Giulia: He's most likely off gazing at the stars. I know he has done that the last few nights.

Vincenzio: He's what? What on earth is he doing that for? He is too old to be doing such nonsense. Why doesn't he get a job? How will he ever support a family?

Giulia: Now, my husband. Do not worry so. Galileo will do just fine. He is very smart and very creative. I am sure that important people will recognize his talents. Besides, look at you. You are able to support nine people. Did you ever think you would do such a thing when you were his age?

Vincenzio: But that is because I took a real job. Remember, at first I studied mathematics and music. I would much rather be a musician than a wool trader. But I knew I must support my family. I grew up.

Narrator 3: Suddenly, there is a loud knock at the door.

Ascanio: Good evening, Mr. and Mrs. Galilei. Is Galileo at home?

Vincenzio: [grumbling] No, you would know where he is better than us.

Ascanio: Being that it is nighttime and he is not home, I think you are right. I bet I know exactly where to find him. Thank you. Good night to you.

Narrator 1: Ascanio is a good friend of Galileo's. Good friends know your habits, good and bad. Ascanio knew he would find Galileo on the treeless hill outside of the city.

Narrator 2: Ascanio did not understand it, but Galileo seemed to be obsessed with things up over his head. Galileo's latest hobby was to spend hours in the dark staring at the stars.

Marina: Ascanio! Hello. Where are you off to?

Ascanio: Looking for Galileo. Come along if you want to.

Narrator 3: Ascanio and Marina find Galileo sitting on the top of the hill, looking up at the moonless sky. The stars are so bright and thick it looks as though someone spattered sparkling white paint across a black canvas.

Marina: [whispering] What is he doing?

Ascanio: Who knows? I gave up trying to figure him out long ago.

Marina: Oh, I bet he is in love. He is gazing at the stars, thinking about a beautiful girl he has fallen in love with.

Ascanio: [looking at her skeptically] Okay, now I think you're the crazy one. Galileo? The only thing he loves is science. He spends so much of his time looking up, I doubt he'd even see a beautiful girl if she walked right up to him.

Galileo: Ascanio, you shouldn't try to sneak up on people. You're not very good at it.

Ascanio: It's a good thing your hearing works well because your eyes seldom look here at ground level.

Marina: What are you doing out here, Galileo?

Galileo: I was watching the stars. When there is no moon like this, the stars are so easy to see. I am keeping an eye on those two stars up there especially. I think they keep changing position.

Discoverers and Inventors Reader's Theater © 2004 Creative Teaching Press

Ascanio: Marina thought you had fallen in love. She imagined you were out here romantically thinking about someone you'd met.

Galileo: What?! Are you crazy?!

Ascanio: That was what I was wondering, although I think maybe the two of you could keep each other company.

Marina: What could possibly be so interesting about the stars?

Galileo: That's just it. I'm not sure they are stars. You see, the stars appear in the same pattern every night. Throughout the year the stars move around the earth, but they stay in the same position to each other.

Marina: Everybody knows that the earth is the center of the universe and everything revolves around it. What does that matter?

Galileo: It matters a lot! Because I believe these two stars are moving. See that larger light there? That is the planet Jupiter. And those two stars keep moving in relation to Jupiter and the other stars. I think they are moons and they are orbiting Jupiter.

Ascanio: Wow, you have been out here too long. [to Marina] Don't get him started. Before you know it, he'll be lecturing us and giving us homework.

Narrator 1: Suddenly, the three young people hear footsteps approaching. Out of the darkness appears Cosimo, a local official who patrols the streets at night to keep the peace.

Cosimo: Galileo, you want to keep such ideas to yourself. Do you know how dangerous it is for you to say such things?

Narrator 2: At this time, the Church is the most powerful authority in Italy. Everyone holds the view that the earth is the center of the universe and everything in the skies revolves around the earth. To say otherwise is heresy.

Narrator 3: Heresy is a crime. A person accused of heresy could be tried and punished.

Galileo: How can the truth be dangerous? I'm not making these things up. It's just what I see.

Cosimo: Just be careful. You know the authorities already know you well. After your behavior at church last week, they are keeping an eye on you.

Marina: Why? What happened last week?

Ascanio: You haven't heard? You must be the only one in town!

Discoverers and Inventors Reader's Theater © 2004 Creative Teaching Press

THINGS ARE LOOKING UP!

Cosimo: We were all attending church. Galileo was sitting with his family, toward the back. As usual, he was staring at the ceiling rather than paying attention to what was happening around him.

Galileo: One of the lamps was slowly swinging back and forth. It caught my attention.

Cosimo: The lamps are hung from the ceiling by a long cord.

Ascanio: Next thing we know, Galileo gets that strange look on his face when he's thinking, and he starts taking his pulse.

Marina: Why? Weren't you feeling well?

Ascanio: Now *that* would have made sense.

Galileo: NO, I noticed that the lamp swung back and forth very regularly. So I was timing each swing. And it gave me an idea.

Cosimo: By this time, several people had noticed that Galileo was not listening to the church service. And so many people were watching Galileo that the bishop became annoyed.

Ascanio: But wait! It gets better. Tell her what you did after church.

Galileo: I experimented. I tied different weights to strings of different lengths and I watched how each swung back and forth. I called these devices pendulums.

Ascanio: Can you imagine? With all the ways to spend your time and he spends his watching swinging weights at the end of a string.

Galileo: Sometimes I did feel a little sleepy, but it was fascinating. It didn't matter how heavy the weight was. The pendulums all had the same swings. And even as the arc of each swing grew shorter, each swing still took the same amount of time. It never got faster or slower.

Marina: But why is that important?

Galileo: I don't know, but I'll think of something. Maybe it could be used to measure time. If I used a very short string, the swings were very fast. If I used a very long string, the swings were slow. But the arcs of the swing were always the same.

Ascanio: [sarcastically] Fascinating.

Cosimo: And then there was the incident at the leaning tower.

Discoverers and Inventors Reader's Theater © 2004 Creative Teaching Press

Marina: What happened there? Don't tell me you had anything to do with the sorry state of that building.

Galileo: Of course not. But it makes the perfect place to conduct experiments . . .

Cosimo: . . . if you're dropping things. He was experimenting with the way things fall. He took some lead balls and some wood balls, in many different sizes, up into the tower.

Galileo: Lead is much heavier than wood, you know.

Ascanio: We do now!

Galileo: Most people believe that heavy objects fall faster than light objects. I didn't think so. I think gravity pulls everything to the earth at the same rate. And I proved it. It didn't matter what balls I dropped, if I let them go at the same time, they all reached the ground at the same time.

Cosimo: You should have seen the crowd. At first people laughed at him and teased him.

Galileo: They weren't laughing in the end. They were in awe!

Marina: Why, they probably thought it was some kind of magic. Galileo, no wonder Cosimo is worried for you. You know what kind of trouble you can get into for practicing magic.

Galileo: Yes, I see your point. You know, it's late. Let's head home.

Narrator 1: Cosimo goes about his duties and the three young people return to their homes.

Vincenzio: Tired of the stars are you?

Galileo: For tonight. I thought I'd come home and work on my latest experiment. It's a tube of metal fixed with a glass lens. It's called a telescope. I didn't actually invent it, but I think I can make it even better.

Vincenzio: A telescope?! What will you possibly use that for? Can it give you a job or make you any money? Oh Galileo, I don't know what to do with you. I fear you will never amount to anything!

RELATED LESSONS

As the Pendulum Swings

OBJECTIVE

Demonstrate how a pendulum works.

ACTIVITY

Explain that Galileo did many experiments with pendulums. He found that a pendulum would swing at a constant rate until it eventually came to a stop. The rate of speed was not affected by the weight attached to the string but only by the length of the string. A pendulum with a short string completes its arc in a shorter time than a pendulum with a long string. Have students work in pairs. Give each pair a **length of string** and a **small ball of modeling clay.** Ask students to tie a knot at one end and mold a ball of clay around this knot. Have one student time a minute on a clock while the other student holds the pendulum and releases the string. Ask students to experiment with the length of the string by changing where they hold the string. Have them release the pendulum and count the number of swings in one minute's time. Discuss the results as a class.

All By Galileo

OBJECTIVE

Familiarize students with the many inventions and ideas created by Galileo.

ACTIVITY

Give each student an **In the Interest of Galileo reproducible (page 33).** Explain to students that the words in the box are all inventions or ideas thought up by Galileo. Have students read each crossword clue and write the correct answer in the box. Then, ask them to use the words to complete the crossword puzzle.

ANSWERS

Down

1. moons of Jupiter
2. compass
4. telescope
6. gravity
7. planets

Across

2. clock
3. magnetism
5. pendulum
8. inclined plane

Name_____   Date _____

In the Interest of Galileo

pendulum	magnetism	clock
inclined plane	planets	telescope
moons of Jupiter	gravity	compass

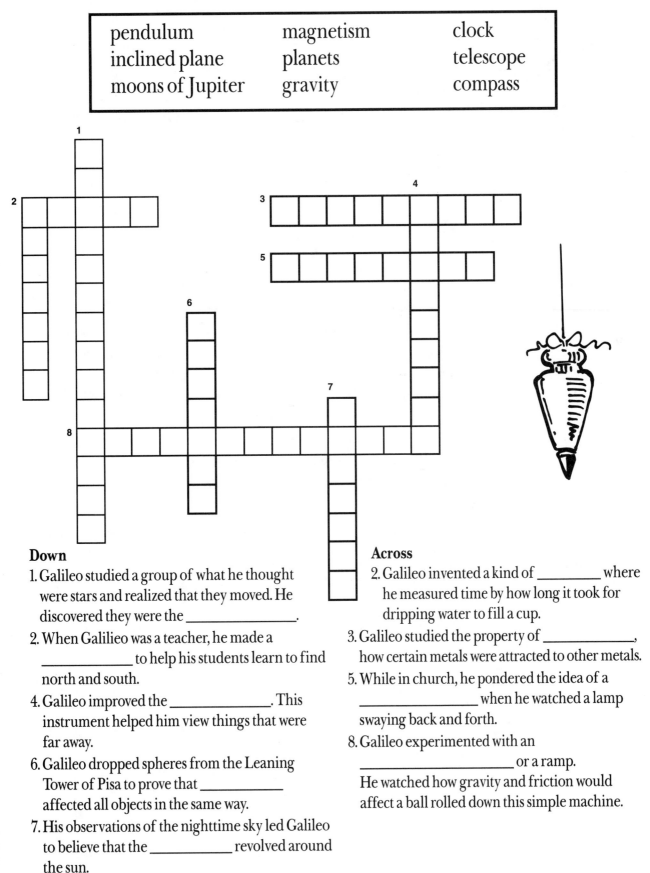

Down

1. Galileo studied a group of what he thought were stars and realized that they moved. He discovered they were the _____.

2. When Galilieo was a teacher, he made a _____ to help his students learn to find north and south.

4. Galileo improved the _____. This instrument helped him view things that were far away.

6. Galileo dropped spheres from the Leaning Tower of Pisa to prove that _____ affected all objects in the same way.

7. His observations of the nighttime sky led Galileo to believe that the _____ revolved around the sun.

Across

2. Galileo invented a kind of _____ where he measured time by how long it took for dripping water to fill a cup.

3. Galileo studied the property of _____, how certain metals were attracted to other metals.

5. While in church, he pondered the idea of a _____ when he watched a lamp swaying back and forth.

8. Galileo experimented with an _____ or a ramp. He watched how gravity and friction would affect a ball rolled down this simple machine.

ISAAC
NEWTON
(1642–1727)

**DISCOVERERS
AND INVENTORS**

VOCABULARY

Discuss each of the following words with students. Then, have students choose one of the words to define and illustrate.

apothecary: a pharmacist

custom: something that members of a group usually do

mechanical: relating to machines or tools

muck out: clean out the waste and straw from an animal stall or barn

omen: something that is thought to be a sign of a good or bad event to come

BACKGROUND

Sir Isaac Newton was one of the greatest minds the world has ever known. His theories and experiments in gravity, motion, light, and calculus are the cornerstones in science today. Throughout his life, he wondered about the world around him. As a young boy, he showed talent with mechanical things, but wasn't a very good student. He tried to help out his mother on the family farm, but he was often so preoccupied with other things that he neglected his duties and was later sent back to school. It wasn't until he was older that he began to work on the theories for which he is famous.

Explain to students that a career in the church was a respected profession and that both Isaac's uncle, Reverend Ayscough, and his late stepfather, Reverend Smith, were preachers.

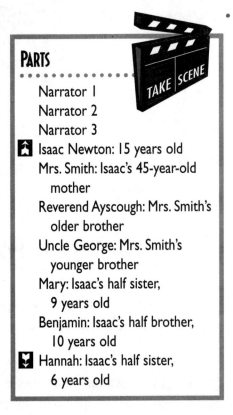

PARTS

Narrator 1

Narrator 2

Narrator 3

Isaac Newton: 15 years old

Mrs. Smith: Isaac's 45-year-old
mother

Reverend Ayscough: Mrs. Smith's
older brother

Uncle George: Mrs. Smith's
younger brother

Mary: Isaac's half sister,
9 years old

Benjamin: Isaac's half brother,
10 years old

Hannah: Isaac's half sister,
6 years old

FLUENCY INSTRUCTION

Have students discuss the ages of the characters to help them reflect the maturity level in their reading. When you read aloud the script for students, have them listen for the following:

• The pace of the reading speeds up when a character is excited. Have students name at least three places where the reading pace will pick up in this script.

• Isaac is very fond of his younger half siblings. When he speaks to them, he is kind and supportive. In turn, the younger children look up to Isaac and want him to interact with them. Have children identify scenes in the story that demonstrate the relationship that Isaac and the children have.

• When adults are exasperated with a child's behavior, they often slow down their speech and clearly say each word to emphasize their point. Have students identify when Mrs. Smith is exasperated with Isaac's behavior and demonstrate how she communicates her feelings through her words.

COMPREHENSION

After you read aloud the script, ask students these questions:

1. Who is Reverend Ayscough?

2. For what reasons did Isaac leave school? Do you agree or disagree with this decision?

3. Why does Uncle George say that he doesn't think Isaac is cut out to be a farmer?

4. Do you think Isaac is a good or bad influence on his younger siblings? Why or why not?

5. If you had seen Isaac jumping from the loft during a storm, what would you have thought?

NOT A FARMER

PARTS

Narrator 1
Narrator 2
Narrator 3
Isaac Newton: 15 years old
Mrs. Smith: Isaac's 45-year-old mother
Reverend Ayscough: Mrs. Smith's older brother
Uncle George: Mrs. Smith's younger brother
Mary: Isaac's half sister, 9 years old
Benjamin: Isaac's half brother, 10 years old
Hannah: Isaac's half sister, 6 years old

Narrator 1: It is the year 1656. A large manor house called Woolsthorpe sits in the countryside of England. This is the childhood home of Isaac Newton.

Narrator 2: Isaac's father died 3 months before he was born. As was the custom of the time, Isaac's mother, Hannah, was urged to remarry quickly. She accepted the proposal of Reverend Barnabas Smith.

Narrator 3: Reverend Smith treated Isaac like his own son, even after his son and two daughters were born. When Reverend Smith died, he even left Isaac some property of his own.

Narrator 1: But 1656 is a difficult time in England. The whole country has its problems. Taxes are very high. Wages are very low. It is hard to find help to harvest crops. Hannah Smith discusses the situation with her brothers, Isaac's uncles.

Mrs. Smith: I don't have a choice anymore. Isaac has to leave his schooling and come home to help me here on the farm.

Reverend: I agree, dear sister. You need the help. Isaac can learn how to run a farm. It is a useful occupation.

Uncle George: I could use his help here, at least until the younger children get older and they can help. Isaac has a good mechanical mind.

Narrator 2: It is the custom of the time that when children reach a certain age, they go away to school.

Narrator 3: Isaac was at school in the nearby village of Grantham. He returned home when his stepfather died to help his mother and Uncle George with the farm.

Narrator 1: So it was decided that Isaac would return home.

Discoverers and Inventors Reader's Theater © 2004 Creative Teaching Press

Narrator 2:	Isaac is much older than his half brother and half sisters, but he enjoys their company and is particularly close to them.
Narrator 3:	They often watch Isaac as he builds strange things and conducts odd experiments.
Mary:	What is that, Isaac?
Isaac:	It's a windmill, Mary. You know, like the one they built down on Gunnerby Road.
Benjamin:	But that one is huge!
Mary:	This one is so small. What will it do?
Isaac:	This one is a model. It is smaller than the real one. I wanted to see how the wind made the paddles turn.
Benjamin:	You are always building something, Isaac. Why?
Isaac:	I don't know. I just like to do it. Don't you like to know how things work?
Benjamin:	No, it's enough for me that they do. I would rather go fish in the stream or hunt rabbit in the woods. That's what I call fun.
Hannah:	I remember when Isaac made that firecracker. That was fun!
Isaac:	Maybe for you! Uncle George was so angry. He made me muck out the barn for that.
Mary:	Can't you make another one? Please, Isaac?
Isaac:	And will you get punished in my place? Besides, I got the supplies from Mr. Clark's apothecary shop when I was at school.
Mary:	How about a kite? Can you make another kite?
Benjamin:	[laughing] Yeah, remember last time?
Hannah:	What happened? I don't remember this.
Isaac:	That's because you are too young. You had to stay with Mama.
Hannah:	Too young! I'm always too young.
Mary:	Isaac made a kite and he showed us how to fly it.
Benjamin:	It was hard to get it in the air at first, but then it almost feels like you have a wild animal at the end of a long string.

NOT A FARMER

Mary: Isaac tied a small lantern to the tail of the kite. We flew the kite for a few more tries.

Benjamin: Then we waited until dark. You were asleep, Hannah.

Isaac: We took the kite out into the empty field by the edge of the village. I lit the lantern and up it went into the dark sky.

Mary: Hannah, it was so funny. The peasants thought it was a comet. They thought the world was coming to an end!

Hannah: But comets are bad omens! I would be afraid, too.

Isaac: Comets are not bad omens. They are just burning objects in the sky. We can see them at night because the sky is dark. But they don't mean anything.

Benjamin: As it was, we all three got into trouble for that one. Uncle George saw us leave and he knew we were up to something.

Isaac: He was right though. If the kite had crashed, we could have started a fire.

Mrs. Smith: [loudly] Boys, girls! Time for supper!

Narrator 1: Isaac and the three children run to the house and wash for supper.

Narrator 2: They are delighted that their uncle, Reverend Ayscough, joins them for dinner.

Narrator 3: By the end of the meal, the weather has changed. A strong wind is beginning to blow.

Reverend: Ah, Hannah, a delightful meal. Thank you for inviting me.

Uncle George: And I agree, sister. [to Isaac] Isaac, the wind is beginning to pick up. The animals need to be put in the barn for the night and the doors need to be shut tight.

Benjamin: Can I help? I want to help Isaac.

Isaac: Not this time, Ben. You stay here in the house. I'll play a game of cards with you when I get back.

Narrator 1: Isaac pulls on his coat and goes out the front door.

Reverend: Isaac is a good lad, Hannah. It is a shame he could not have stayed in school.

Mrs. Smith: I agree with you, but what else could we do? I need the help here, at least until Benjamin and Mary are a little older.

Discoverers and Inventors Reader's Theater © 2004 Creative Teaching Press

NOT A FARMER

Uncle George: Sometimes I think he might be better suited to schooling than farming.

Reverend: Why is that?

Uncle George: Isaac is a thinker. Yes, he likes to build things, but often I find him daydreaming about the funniest things when he should be doing his chores.

Mrs. Smith: He is indeed absentminded. Just last week he was leading the brown mare down the road to the front pasture. He began thinking about something odd.

Uncle George: The horse slipped out of its bridle and trotted back to the stable alone. Isaac was so deep in thought he didn't notice.

Mrs. Smith: We thought something had happened to him. When we caught up with him, he was still holding the bridle. He didn't even know the horse was no longer behind him!

Mary: Mama? Has Isaac come back from the barn yet?

Mrs. Smith: He isn't back yet?

Benjamin: No, and he promised to play a game with me.

Uncle George: He's been gone a long time. He should have finished by now.

Mrs. Smith: Perhaps something has happened. This strong wind can knock a person down.

Narrator 2: The whole family is so concerned that they head for the barn. Immediately, they can tell that the barn doors still stand wide open. Isaac is nowhere in sight.

Benjamin: There he is!

Reverend: Where, lad?

Benjamin: Just inside, up in the loft.

Narrator 3: At that moment, just as a large gust of wind pushes them closer, they watch in amazement as they see Isaac jump from the loft and land in the soft hay below.

Mrs. Smith: Isaac Newton! What are you doing?

Uncle George: Isaac, why aren't these doors shut? And why are the animals still outside?

Isaac: [excitedly] Oh, I forgot. But wait! Look at what I have discovered. I am measuring the force of the wind.

Discoverers and Inventors Reader's Theater © 2004 Creative Teaching Press

NOT A FARMER

Mrs. Smith: You're what??

Isaac: The wind! I jump just as the wind blows. The stronger the gust, the farther I go before I hit the ground! Isn't that amazing?

Benjamin: I want to try it.

Mrs. Smith: Oh, Isaac, what am I going to do with you? Benjamin, stay here!

Uncle George: [laughing] I don't think Isaac is cut out to be a farmer.

Reverend: Yes, I agree. Hannah, you may want to reconsider your decision. I can make arrangements for Isaac to return to school.

Mrs. Smith: Yes, I think you are right. Isaac! Stop this instant and get this barn closed up. Then, come into the house. I believe we have your future to discuss.

Discoverers and Inventors Reader's Theater © 2004 Creative Teaching Press

RELATED LESSONS

Magic by Inertia

OBJECTIVE
Demonstrate how inertia works on an object

ACTIVITY
Explain that the law of inertia states that all matter tends to remain at rest unless it is acted upon by an outside force. Divide the class into pairs, and have each pair experience inertia using a **nickel**, a **drinking glass**, and a **square of cardboard** big enough to cover the mouth of the glass. Have students place the cardboard over the mouth of the glass and set the nickel in the center of the cardboard. Ask students to give the edge of the cardboard a quick snap with their finger. If they hit the cardboard right on the edge and don't flip it up, they will be able to watch the nickel drop straight down into the glass. This is because their finger forces the cardboard into motion, but gravity still pulls the coin down.

Life of Newton

OBJECTIVE
Research the important dates in the life of Isaac Newton and complete a timeline.

ACTIVITY
Give each student a **Newton Timeline reproducible (page 42)**. Explain that this timeline gives the years when important events took place in Isaac Newton's life. Have students research the life of Isaac Newton in **books** or on the **Internet**. Ask them to complete the timeline by adding information for each date. Encourage students to include detailed descriptions of the events and write in complete sentences.

ANSWERS
1642 Isaac Newton is born

1661 Enters Cambridge University

1666 Uses prism to show light is made up of spectrum

1668 Invents the reflecting telescope

1669 Appointed professor of mathematics at Cambridge

1672 Announces the law of gravitation

1678 Announces his three laws of motion

1705 Knighted by the queen

1727 Newton dies

Name_____ Date _____

Newton Timeline

Directions: Write complete sentences that describe an event in Isaac Newton's life in each year listed below.

1642 _____

_____

1661 _____

_____

1666 _____

_____

1668 _____

_____

1669 _____

_____

1672 _____

_____

1678 _____

_____

1705 _____

_____

1727 _____

_____

Discoverers and Inventors Reader's Theater © 2004 Creative Teaching Press

LOUIS PASTEUR (1822–1895)

DISCOVERERS AND INVENTORS

VOCABULARY

Discuss each of the following words with students. Then, have students discuss why each word might be important to understanding the script.

ascent: the act of going or moving up

eccentric: odd or unusual in appearance or behavior

expedition: a journey made for a definite purpose

Monsieur: (meh SYUR) the French address for "Mister"

nevertheless: however, in spite of that

BACKGROUND

Louis Pasteur was a careful and thoughtful scientist. His career began with the study of crystals and the way they are formed. Then, he was asked to help a winery find out why their wine kept spoiling. He determined that the yeast used to make wine was a living organism, and he found that microbes that caused the wine to spoil could be killed by heat. This process is called pasteurization in his honor. He was determined to find out the cause for many of the diseases of the day. He devoted his life to studying the microbes that caused rabies, cholera, and anthrax and to finding a vaccine for each.

PARTS

Narrator 1

Narrator 2

⭐ Louis (loo EE) Pasteur (pass TOUR): French chemist

François (fran SWAH): a trail guide, 28 years old

André (AHN dray): a trail guide, 31 years old

Peter: a trail guide, 18 years old

Leeuwenhoek (LAY wen hook): inventor of the compound microscope

Greta: 20-year-old woman

⭐ Marta: 24-year-old woman

FLUENCY INSTRUCTION

Have students discuss the ages of the characters to help them reflect the maturity level in their reading. When you read aloud the script for students, have them listen for the following:

- Sometimes characters interrupt each other. Have students practice reading the dialogue between André and Peter where they interrupt each other on the first page of the script.
- When characters are preoccupied, they may speak haltingly if they are interrupted. Demonstrate how Louis would say this line if he were interrupted in his work: **Louis:** *Uh, what? Oh, good morning, um, François, is it?* Point out how the commas help show how halting his speech is.
- Words in all capital letters show that the character is yelling or talking very loudly. Have students identify where a character is yelling in the script.
- When a character is excited, he or she will speak rapidly and loudly. Have students find where Leeuwenhoek speaks excitedly and practice reading these lines in a rapid and loud manner.

COMPREHENSION

After you read aloud the script, ask students these questions:

1. Who is Leeuwenhoek?

2. Why are two of the guides afraid of Louis Pasteur?

3. What does Leeuwenhoek do that makes the women think he is eccentric?

4. Do you think the expedition to Mont Blanc was worthwhile? Why or why not?

5. Why was the invention of the microscope important to the study of germs?

6. Why is the line about bottling water humorous?

THE AIR COLLECTOR

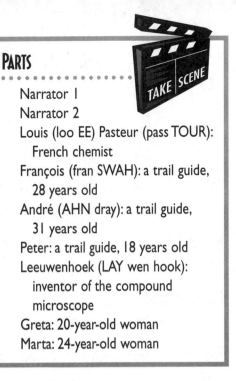

PARTS

Narrator 1
Narrator 2
Louis (loo EE) Pasteur (pass TOUR):
   French chemist
François (fran SWAH): a trail guide,
   28 years old
André (AHN dray): a trail guide,
   31 years old
Peter: a trail guide, 18 years old
Leeuwenhoek (LAY wen hook):
   inventor of the compound
   microscope
Greta: 20-year-old woman
Marta: 24-year-old woman

Narrator 1: Our story takes place atop a high mountain in the Alps, Mont Blanc, in 1859.

Narrator 2: A small party of individuals begins the day in camp on the side of the mountain. One man is off by himself. He is surrounded by a collection of odd-shaped bottles. Three other men are busy around a campfire.

François: Such a beautiful day! Not a cloud in the sky.

André: Not for now. But you know what it is like up here in the mountains. The weather can change in an instant.

Peter: How true. I remember an expedition a few years back where it started off just this sunny and fifteen minutes later . . .

André: . . . it was snowing. Yes, yes, you've told that story many times, Peter.

Peter: Actually, I don't think I have. It's just many times the story ends that way here on Mont Blanc.

François: Nevertheless, you would think Mr. Pasteur would be eager to get started.

André: Go ask him what he plans to do.

Peter: Not me. He confuses me with all this talk about germs. It makes my skin crawl. François, you are youngest, you go ask.

François: Oh all right. Monsieur Pasteur does not bother me. I find him rather interesting.

André: Interesting?! That's one way to describe him. He pays the bills and he takes our advice about the mountain. But I agree with Peter. His talk of germs is very strange indeed.

Peter: Go on with you then, François. We will begin our preparations. Find out when Monsieur Pasteur wants to head up the mountain.

Narrator 1: François needed no more encouragement. He liked nothing more than talking with this unusual man.

Narrator 2: François liked the scientist's experiments. He liked to hear how precise he was. Francois thought that someday he might like to do experiments too.

François: Good morning, Monsieur Pasteur. Are those bottles what you need?

Louis: Uh, what? Oh, good morning, um, François, is it?

François: Yes, sir.

Louis: The bottles are fine, I think. We will find out today.

François: That's why I am here. The others would like to know what your plans are today.

Louis: It looks like a good day for the mountain. I think I should like to collect my samples, if you all agree.

François: I believe we do. Monsieur Pasteur, I don't understand. These bottles look exactly like the ones you had before.

Louis: They are like the ones I had before. The other bottles were ruined when I couldn't get them sealed again. It was the lamp that caused me problems. The flame was not strong enough and I couldn't melt the glass fast enough in the strong winds on the mountains.

François: This lamp should be better. It burns much hotter. Is this another experiment about germs, sir?

Louis: Indeed it is.

François: I don't quite understand these germs. Did you discover them?

Louis: No, I did not. That was done well before my time. Let me tell you about a man named Anton van Leeuwenhoek. He invented the microscope.

Discoverers and Inventors Reader's Theater © 2004 Creative Teaching Press

THE AIR COLLECTOR

Narrator 1: François was pleased. Monsieur Pasteur was doing what François was hoping he'd do: tell one of his interesting stories.

Narrator 2: Louis told the story with so much detail that François felt as if he were there, transported back in time, watching the event happen for the first time.

Narrator 1: François could picture Leeuwenhoek bent over his microscope examining the millions of tiny creatures swimming around in a single drop of rainwater.

Leeuwenhoek: This is amazing! Come see, come see!

Greta: I beg your pardon, sir. Are you speaking to us?

Marta: [softly to the woman] Be careful, Greta. He seems rather dangerous.

Greta: Oh, it's all right. It's only our neighbor. He's a bit eccentric, but he's harmless.

Leeuwenhoek: I beg your pardon, ladies. But I just have to tell someone about my discovery.

Marta: And what would that be?

Leeuwenhoek: Creatures! Little creatures! In a drop of water! Here. Look at them. Look through the top of this instrument here.

Greta: I don't see anything. And what would be small enough to fit in there anyway?

Marta: Let me try. Oh. Oh! I see what you mean! Greta, you have to look closely. They look like little worms swimming about.

Greta: Oh, yes. Now I do see. You are right, sir, this is an amazing discovery.

Leeuwenhoek: That's not my discovery. I already knew about those little creatures. It's what happens to them that is my discovery.

Marta: What happens to them?

Leeuwenhoek: They stop moving after I drink very hot coffee!

Greta: Excuse me?

Leeuwenhoek: They stop moving!

Greta: But how would your drinking coffee stop them from moving?

Leeuwenhoek: Oh, I forgot a step. You see, I make a scraping off of my teeth. And when I look at it under the slide, there are little creatures moving about. But after I drink hot coffee, I scrape my teeth again. This time they are no longer moving!

Greta: That's disgusting! You mean to tell us that those little things came out of your MOUTH?!

Leeuwenhoek: Yes, yes! I don't know what they are, but they don't like hot coffee!

Marta: Let's get out of here, Greta. I think the man may have creatures in his brain as well.

Narrator 1: A sudden gust of cold wind brings François back to the present. He shakes his head to clear his thoughts.

François: I love your stories, Monsieur Pasteur.

Louis: But they are not just stories, François. What Leeuwenhoek saw were germs or bacteria. They are all around us, or at least that's what I'm trying to prove.

André: François, I thought I told you to find out what Monsieur Pasteur's plans were. You've been gone a long time.

Louis: I am ready to go when you are, André.

Narrator 2: So the little party begins the ascent up Mont Blanc.

Narrator 1: When they reach the edge of the glacier, Louis Pasteur asks them to stop. He begins unpacking his supplies.

Louis: This is perfect. I can collect my samples here.

Peter: Is there anything you would like us to do?

Louis: No, no. I think I can do it. Rest yourselves. We'll have to descend the mountain in a short while.

Narrator 1: The three men sit down to watch a short distance away. From there, they watch the strangest ritual.

André: Look what he does. He snaps off the tip of each bottle.

François: Can you hear that hiss? The air rushes into the bottle.

Discoverers and Inventors Reader's Theater © 2004 Creative Teaching Press

THE AIR COLLECTOR

Peter: What? What does he do now? He melts the glass with the lamp and seals the bottles shut again. But what did he collect? There is nothing in the bottle.

François: There is air!

André: Air? He's collecting air? We climbed all this way to collect air?

Louis: Ah, my good sirs. I am finished. I have collected what I came for.

Peter: You collected air? You hiked all this way for air? Don't they have air where you live?

Louis: Of course, but not this air. This air is pure and has little dust. I want to compare it to air from other spots.

André: Pure air! I don't believe it. These city people are crazy. Next thing you know, they'll want to bottle our water.

RELATED LESSONS

Growing Crystals

OBJECTIVE

Grow, observe, and compare different types of crystals.

ACTIVITY

Explain that Louis Pasteur began his scientific career studying crystals and how they formed. Explain to students that they will set up this experiment to watch crystals form over a long period of time. Give each small group a **glass jar with a wide mouth**, a **strip of black construction paper**, and **1 cup (250 mL) of water**. Add one of the following to each group's jar: **6 tablespoons (90 mL) salt, 6 tablespoons sugar, or 6 tablespoons Epsom salts**. Have groups pour in the water and swirl to dissolve. Have groups use a **white gel pen** to write the type of material in the jar on the paper strip. Place the strip in the water, and press it against the inside of the jar. Set the jars in a place where they won't be disturbed. Ask students to observe the jar over several weeks. Once crystals form on the paper strips, have groups compare the size and shape of the crystals. Note: Provide **magnifying lenses** if students need help seeing the crystals.

Pasteur Word Match

OBJECTIVE

Match words to their definitions.

ACTIVITY

Give each student a **Louis Pasteur Word Match reproducible (page 51)**. Explain that the words in the word box are all related to the research of and discoveries made by Louis Pasteur. Have students read through the words. Then, have them read the definitions below. Ask students to write the word that matches each definition. Encourage them to use a **dictionary or encyclopedia** to help define words with which they are unfamiliar. Have students compare their answers.

ANSWERS

1. bacillus
2. spontaneous generation
3. bacteria
4. pasteurization
5. fermentation

6. microbes
7. yeasts
8. antibiotic
9. silkworm disease and spoiled wine
10. vaccine

Name_____   Date _____

Louis Pasteur Word Match

bacillus	yeasts	silkworm disease and
microbes	fermentation	spoiled wine
bacteria	vaccine	antibiotic
spontaneous generation		pasteurization

1. _____ bacteria that are rod-shaped

2. _____ a theory that states that living things can spring forth from nonliving material; this theory was proven wrong by Louis Pasteur

3. _____ tiny one-celled organisms, some of which can cause diseases

4. _____ a process by which heat is applied to kill microbes

5. _____ a chemical process by which sugar in a liquid turns into alcohol and a gas

6. _____ very tiny living organisms; bacteria are an example of these

7. _____ tiny one-celled fungi that grow rapidly; they are used to make bread grow and turn juice into wine

8. _____ a substance that kills germs or stops their growth

9. _____ two problems that were solved by the efforts of Louis Pasteur

10. _____ a preparation of weak or dead microorganisms that is put into the body and protects against infection by a specific disease

Discoverers and Inventors Reader's Theater © 2004 Creative Teaching Press

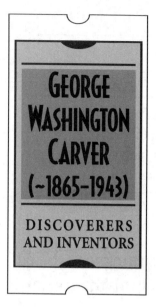

GEORGE
WASHINGTON
CARVER
(~1865–1943)

DISCOVERERS
AND INVENTORS

VOCABULARY

Discuss each of the following words with students. Then, have students identify the word they best understand and least understand. Have volunteers use the word they best understand in a sentence. (You may choose to have more than one example for a given word.)

farmstead: a farm, including its fields and buildings

horticultural: having to do with the cultivation of plants

land sakes!: an exclamation similar to *Oh, my!*

porridge: a food made by boiling meal, such as oatmeal, in milk or water until it is thick

proboscis: a slender tubular feeding organ on certain insects

BACKGROUND

George Washington Carver was born sometime around 1865. His exact birthday is not known because he was born the son of a slave at the end of the Civil War. Records for births to slave parents were not always kept. George's mother, Mary, was owned by the Carvers in Diamond Grove, Missouri. Even though the Carvers were opposed to slavery, they purchased Mary to help out on their busy farm. During a raid by slavery supporters, George, his mother, and his brother Jim were kidnapped. The Carvers were able to rescue George and Jim, but George never saw his mother again. The Carvers raised the boys like family, educating them and giving them their last name. It was during this time that George began to show an interest and talent in taking care of plants. He often answered questions for the neighbors and became known as the "plant doctor." As an adult, he is best-known for the products he created from the peanut and the sweet potato.

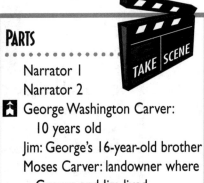

PARTS

Narrator 1

Narrator 2

George Washington Carver:
   10 years old

Jim: George's 16-year-old brother

Moses Carver: landowner where
   George and Jim lived

Susan Carver: wife of
   Moses Carver

Silas Morgan: the Carvers'
   65-year-old neighbor

Mary Hodges: the Carvers'
   37-year-old neighbor

Tom Wilson: the Carvers'
   33-year-old neighbor

FLUENCY INSTRUCTION

Have students discuss the ages of the characters to help them reflect the maturity level in their reading. When you read aloud the script for students, have them listen for the following:

- George and his brother are much younger than the other characters. As children, their voices will be higher pitched and they will speak faster than the adults.

- Words in italic type signify that emphasis should be placed on those words. For example, in the sentence "He *is* such an odd child," the word *is* should be emphasized. Have students take turns repeating the sentence, each time emphasizing one of the following words: *he, such, odd,* and *child.* Discuss how the meaning of the sentence changes when a different word is emphasized each time.

- When Silas asks for George he is a bit embarrassed to tell Moses why he needs him. Have students experiment with how to read his lines to show embarrassment in his voice.

- Your pace and pitch is fairly steady for any of the narrator lines. Remind students that while they want to keep their voices interesting, the narrators should not convey too much emotion because they are not part of the action or one of the characters.

COMPREHENSION

After you read aloud the script, ask students these questions:

1. Where does this story take place?

2. Summarize what happens in the story.

3. How is George like his brother Jim? How is he different?

4. Do you think George's advice to the neighbors will work? Why or why not?

5. There are lines that repeat throughout the story. What are these lines and why do you think the author used this technique?

ODD, BUT SMART

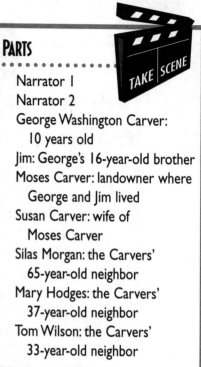
Narrator 1: The year is 1875. Outside the town of Diamond Grove, Missouri, there is a small farmstead.

Narrator 2: This is the home of Moses and Susan Carver. Moses Carver sits on the front porch, playing a violin. His pet rooster, Hubert, perches on the back of his chair, not quite sure of the noise that is coming from the instrument.

Narrator 1: Moses pauses for a moment.

Moses: Susan, have you seen George?

Susan: No, I haven't, dear. After he finished his porridge, he took off out the door. Jim is in the back feeding the hens.

Moses: Did George say where he was going?

Susan: I asked, but he didn't say. I bet he is out in his secret garden. He is embarrassed to let us know he has it.

Moses: Why is that? I am proud that he has taken such an interest in things horticultural.

Susan: I don't know, dear. I don't try to figure him out. He is such an odd child.

Moses: But very smart, he is.

Narrator 1: Moses Carver sets down his violin and walks around to the back of the house. Hubert the rooster follows behind.

Narrator 2: Jim, George's older brother, is just shutting up the henhouse door.

Moses: Jim, have you seen that younger brother of yours? We have not seen him since breakfast.

Discoverers and Inventors Reader's Theater © 2004 Creative Teaching Press

Jim: I stopped trying to keep track of that kid long ago, sir. Undoubtedly, he is somewhere watching the insects fly or the plants grow.

Moses: He *is* such an odd child . . .

Jim: But I give him credit. He is smarter than I'll ever be.

Narrator 1: Moses begins to walk into the woods, the rooster still trailing behind.

Narrator 2: After a short distance, he spots a young boy lying on his stomach in the grass, staring intently at a butterfly on a stem. The boy is ten years old, but he is very small for his age.

Moses: There you are, George. What are you up to?

George: Oh, hello, Mr. Carver. Oops, you scared it off.

Moses: Scared what off?

George: The butterfly. I was watching this butterfly. Did you know they have a long coiled proboscis, and they roll it out to sip up the nectar from a flower?

Moses: Land sakes, George. No, I did not. Did you learn that just watching a butterfly?

George: Not just now. I noticed it a long time ago. You can learn a lot from watching the butterflies.

Moses: That's sort of a strange pet to have there, George.

George: I don't know, sir. I don't think it is any stranger than having a rooster for a pet.

Moses: Good point, George.

Narrator 1: Moses leaves George to his observations and strolls back to the front porch, playing his violin. Just then, his neighbor to the south, Silas Morgan, arrives.

Moses: Good morning, Silas. What brings you to our farm so early in the day?

Silas: Morning, Moses. I have this here sickly plant. Wanted to find out what was wrong with it.

Moses: Hmm, don't know. Does look pretty bad though.

Silas: Sorry, Moses. I wasn't here to ask you. I was here to ask your George. He has such a way with plants, you know.

Moses: Oh, yes, I see. He is a rather odd child, isn't he?

ODD, BUT SMART

Silas:	Maybe, but he sure is smart.
Susan:	Good morning, Silas.
Silas:	Good morning, ma'am. I'm here to see George. Is he about?
Susan:	George? You'll find him if you follow this path a bit. Hasn't done anything wrong, has he?
Silas:	Oh no, no. I, uh, just need to ask him a question.
Narrator 2:	Silas follows the path until he comes to the clearing in the woods. George is so intent on watching a trail of ants that Silas almost trips over him.
Silas:	Whoa, sorry there, George. I didn't see you.
George:	Hi, Mr. Morgan.
Silas:	George, I need your help. I have this here plant and it is doing poorly. You sure are good with plants. Could you see if maybe you know what is wrong with it?
Narrator 1:	George takes the plant from Mr. Morgan and begins to examine it, humming to himself all the while.
Narrator 2:	Meanwhile, back at the house, the neighbor to the north, Tom Wilson, comes up the drive.
Tom:	Hello there, Moses. I'm surprised not to see you busy at work this time of year.
Susan:	I was just coming here to find out why that was myself, Tom!
Moses:	Okay, okay, I was just taking a little rest here. Good morning, Tom. You're about awfully early. What can we do for you?
Tom:	Nothing actually. I thought I might speak to young George if he's not too busy.
Moses:	George again? That boy sure is popular.
Jim:	What does everyone want with George?
Tom:	George seems to know things about plants that nobody else knows. I need to ask his advice. He may be young …
Jim:	And he is sort of odd …

Discoverers and Inventors Reader's Theater © 2004 Creative Teaching Press

Susan:	But he's very smart. Sure, Tom. Just follow the path into the woods a bit. You'll probably see Silas Morgan there, too.
Tom:	Thank you.
Narrator 1:	So Tom also goes down the path and comes across George and Silas Morgan.
George:	So you see, Mr. Morgan, just mash up some of the bugs and some water. Spray the whole thing on any plants where you find more bugs. They'll move away.
Silas:	Thank you, George. Hello there, Tom. What brings you here?
Tom:	Hello to you, Silas. From the sounds of it, the same thing that brought you here. I need some advice about my sweet potato crop. Thought maybe George here could help.
Silas:	If anyone can help you with your sweet potato crop, it will be George.
Narrator 2:	Tom begins to explain to George about his sweet potato crop and Silas sticks around in the hopes that he may learn something, too.
Narrator 1:	As George listens to Tom Wilson's crop problem, yet another neighbor, Mary Hodges, who lives to the east, approaches Moses Carver as he loads up the wagon.
Mary:	Good day to you, Mr. Carver. I hate to bother you when you are busy yourself, but George has been such a help to me in the past and …
Moses:	Let me guess, you need help with a plant.
Mary:	No … actually, I have a question about a particularly nasty bug I keep finding on my squash plants.
Susan:	[to Moses] At this rate, you won't have to do any work at all, Moses. Mary, you'll find George down the path in the clearing. You can't miss him. He's there with Tom Wilson and Silas Morgan already.
Mary:	Really? Seems I'm not the only one who relies on George's advice then, am I?
Narrator 2:	So Mary Hodges starts down the path and soon she joins up with the others.
Mary:	Hello, Tom. Hello, Silas. George, I do need your help. I have this pesky bug that I keep finding on my squash plants. Do you think you might know what it is? Can you think of a way to get rid of it?
Narrator 1:	As the three adults listen to George's explanations, Jim, Moses, and Susan begin to get curious.

Odd, but Smart

Susan: For being so young, an awful lot of people seek out George's advice, don't they?

Moses: I wonder what he could be telling them? I think we should go investigate this for ourselves.

Narrator 2: So all three people start down the path themselves. They arrive just as George is pointing out a strange-looking insect.

Mary: What a creepy-looking insect. What is that thing, George?

George: It's a praying mantis. It may be creepy looking, but it causes you no harm.

Silas: And you say this is actually a good bug?

George: Yes! It eats the bugs that bother your crops. You don't want to kill these just because they look funny. They actually help you. However, they tend to eat all bugs, good or bad.

Mary: It's funny. I never really thought of a bug as good or bad before.

Susan: George, I had no idea that during all this time you spend in the woods you were learning.

Jim: It's almost like he has been going to school out here.

Tom: George gives me more information than I can find in books.

Susan: How about we all take a break and go have some lunch. Tom, Silas, Mary, you join us, too.

Narrator 1: As the adults walk away from the clearing, Jim throws his arm about his little brother's shoulders and grins broadly.

Jim: You know, George, you're awfully little, and sometimes I think you're a little odd, but I am right proud of how smart you are!

George: I know, big brother! I know.

RELATED LESSONS

Biography Sequencing

OBJECTIVE
Take notes from a biography and place the notes in sequential order.

ACTIVITY
Divide the class into pairs. Give each pair a copy of *A Pocketful of Goobers* by Barbara Mitchell (Carolrhoda Books) and **ten large index cards.** Ask pairs to read the story and write an important event on each index card. Have them place a **colored dot sticker** on the back of each card so all the cards can be identified as one set and mix them up. Once all pairs have written their note cards, have pairs trade cards. Have students place the cards in sequential order. Encourage students to compare their results as a class.

Peanut Product Word Search

OBJECTIVE
Investigate the variety of products George Washington Carver created from peanuts.

ACTIVITY
Give each student a **Peanut Product Parade reproducible (page 60).** Explain that this is just a small list of the products George Washington Carver created from peanuts. Have students look for and circle all 20 products in the puzzle. Have them compare their completed puzzles. To extend the activity, tell students that Carver also experimented with a variety of products created from the sweet potato. Ask them to research these sweet potato creations and make a list to share with the class.

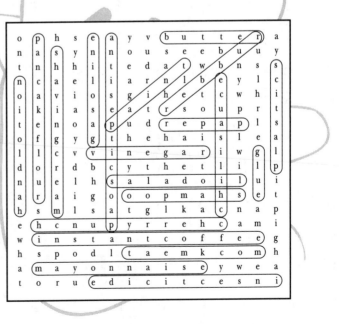

Peanut Product Parade

Directions: Find and circle the products George Washington Carver created from peanuts in the puzzle below.

antiseptic soap	chili sauce	mayonnaise	insecticide
hand lotion	glue	pancake flour	salad oil
shampoo	vinegar	rubber	shaving cream
paint	mock meat	paper	cherry punch
butter	instant coffee	plastics	gasoline

```
o  p  h  s  e  a  y  v  b  u  t  t  e  r  a
n  a  s  y  n  n  o  u  s  e  e  b  u  u  y
t  n  h  h  i  t  e  d  a  t  w  b  n  s  s
n  c  a  e  l  i  a  r  n  l  b  e  y  l  c
o  a  v  i  o  s  g  i  h  e  t  c  w  h  i
i  k  i  a  s  e  a  t  r  s  o  u  p  r  t
t  e  n  o  a  p  u  d  r  e  p  a  p  l  s
o  f  g  y  g  t  h  e  h  a  i  s  l  e  a
l  l  c  v  v  i  n  e  g  a  r  i  w  g  l
d  o  r  d  b  c  y  t  h  e  t  l  i  l  p
n  u  e  l  h  s  a  l  a  d  o  i  l  u  i
a  r  a  i  g  o  o  o  p  m  a  h  s  e  t
h  s  m  l  s  a  t  g  l  k  a  c  n  a  p
e  h  c  n  u  p  y  r  r  e  h  c  a  m  i
w  i  n  s  t  a  n  t  c  o  f  f  e  e  g
h  s  p  o  d  l  t  a  e  m  k  c  o  m  h
a  m  a  y  o  n  n  a  i  s  e  y  w  e  a
t  o  r  u  e  d  i  c  i  t  c  e  s  n  i
```

Discoverers and Inventors Reader's Theater © 2004 Creative Teaching Press

VOCABULARY

Discuss each of the following words with students. Then, have volunteers pantomime the meaning of each word in some way.

bickering: quarreling about something unimportant

coax: to persuade

electrometer: an instrument for measuring the voltage of electricity

embedded: fixed firmly in a surrounding substance

physicist: a scientist who specializes in the study of matter and energy

radioactive: to have a property by which certain chemical elements give off energy as rays

BACKGROUND

Marie Curie was born Marie Salomee Sklodowska on November 7, 1867, in Poland. At the time, Poland was a part of the Russian Empire. Higher education was not available to women. Students in Poland had to learn in Russian as teachers were not allowed to teach in their native Polish language. However, Marie worked very hard and was accepted into the Sorbonne in Paris, France, where she met her husband, Pierre Curie. They both were hard workers who spent a great deal of their time in the laboratory, although they made time to raise a family. The Curies shared a Nobel Prize in 1903 for the discovery of radium, a radioactive element.

PARTS

Narrator 1

Narrator 2

★ Marie Curie: 29-year-old scientist

Bronya: Marie's 34-year-old sister

Joseph: Marie's 32-year-old brother

Hela: Marie's 30-year-old sister

Father: Marie's father

Lena: 7-year-old daughter of Bronya, Marie's niece

⚑ Casimir: 10-year-old son of Bronya, Marie's nephew

FLUENCY INSTRUCTION

Have students discuss the ages of the characters to help them reflect the maturity level in their reading. When you read aloud the script for students, have them listen for the following:

• The children in the story are much younger than the youngest adult. Have students identify how the adults' voices change when they talk to the children and when they talk to each other.

• Your voice chokes and your speech slows when Marie gets emotional when she sees her father.

• When the family begins to bicker, their voices get louder and take on a sarcastic tone. Say a line in a plain tone of voice, then repeat it in a sarcastic tone. Have students compare how the meaning of the line changes.

• Your voice rises at the end of a question such as on the line **Father:** *Hello, my dear Marie. How are you? And how is Pierre?*

• The pace picks up when the children are excited. Have students identify two places in the story where the pace will pick up.

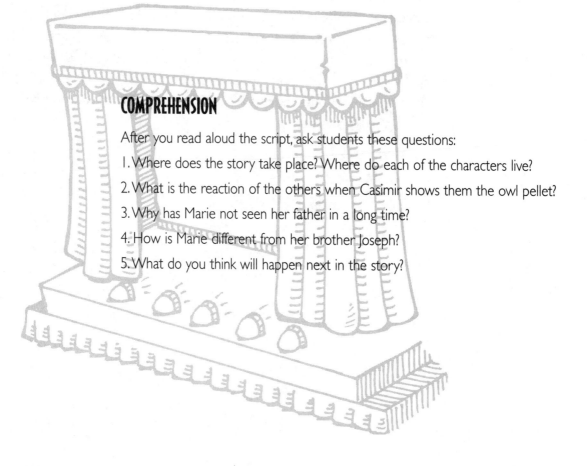

COMPREHENSION

After you read aloud the script, ask students these questions:

1. Where does the story take place? Where do each of the characters live?

2. What is the reaction of the others when Casimir shows them the owl pellet?

3. Why has Marie not seen her father in a long time?

4. How is Marie different from her brother Joseph?

5. What do you think will happen next in the story?

Picnic in Paris

PARTS

Narrator 1
Narrator 2
Marie Curie: 29-year-old scientist
Bronya: Marie's 34-year-old sister
Joseph: Marie's 32-year-old brother
Hela: Marie's 30-year-old sister
Father: Marie's father
Lena: 7-year-old daughter of Bronya, Marie's niece
Casimir: 10-year-old son of Bronya, Marie's nephew

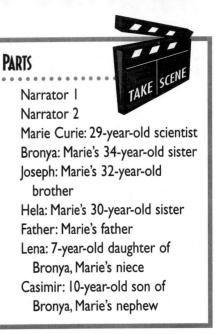

Narrator 1: It is a beautiful spring day in 1896. Outside of the city of Paris, the Sklodowska family has reunited for a picnic.

Narrator 2: This is the family of Marie Curie. Marie moved to Paris in 1891 to study at the Sorbonne.

Narrator 1: Marie later met and married Pierre Curie, another physicist. Together, they share a laboratory, conduct experiments, and teach.

Narrator 2: Marie decided to leave her experiments for a little while to spend some time with her family.

Lena and Casimir: Aunt Marie! Aunt Marie! Oh, Mama, look. She has finally arrived.

Marie: Hello, Lena. Hello, Casimir. It is so good to see you! My, look at how you have grown. Casimir, before too long, you will be as tall as me.

Casimir: I think I am almost as tall as you now.

Marie: My dear sisters. How happy I am to see you.

Hela: And I am so glad to see you as well.

Bronya: Marie, it is so sad. We live in the same city and yet I see so little of you.

Marie: I know, I know. I am sorry. It's just my studies, my teaching, and my experiments take up so much of my time. [choking] Oh, Father! No, don't get up. I am so pleased you made this long journey to see me.

Father: Hello, my dear Marie. How are you? And how is Pierre?

Marie: I am well, and Pierre is fine. He wanted to be here, but we are making good progress with our experiments. We couldn't afford the time for both of us to be here.

PICNIC IN PARIS

Hela: Marie, you look tired. Are you sure you are not working too hard? I know how hard you study.

Narrator 1: Marie had been born in Poland in 1867. At that time, Poland was ruled by Russia. Russian teachers replaced Polish teachers. Russian books were used in the schools.

Narrator 2: If the Polish people complained, they were put in prison. But many people secretly sent their children to Polish schools to learn about their Polish heritage.

Narrator 1: Marie and her siblings were always eager to learn and studied hard.

Narrator 2: Marie always studied much harder than anyone else.

Marie: Don't worry, Hela. Yes, we work very hard, but we also rest when we can.

Joseph: [teasing] I know you, Marie. Pierre probably wants to rest, but you won't let him. Always cracking a whip over his head, you are!

Marie: [smiling] No, Joseph. Sometimes I have to make Pierre stop. He is a hard worker. Unlike you!

Hela: Yes, Joseph. Don't assume that since we had to coax you to work, that everyone else is just like you!

Bronya: Listen to you all! And don't give my children ideas. Try being the oldest in the family. Then let's talk about who works the hardest.

Father: I don't believe my ears! Lena, Casimir, can you believe your elders? They bicker like small children.

Bronya: Even I don't bicker like that!

Casimir: Humph!

Joseph: Okay. Stop. Everyone. Even the children are bickering now. We shouldn't waste our precious time together arguing about things in the past.

Lena: Aunt Marie, Casimir says that you study and experiment with rocks. Is that true? Why does a person study rocks?

Marie: I don't exactly study rocks. Although there are many special things about rocks.

Casimir: Aunt Marie and Uncle Pierre study special kinds of rocks. Their rocks glow!

Discoverers and Inventors Reader's Theater © 2004 Creative Teaching Press

PICNIC IN PARIS

Lena: Really, Aunt Marie?

Marie: Not exactly. The rocks I am studying contain something that is radioactive. They give off radiation. I can't see the radiation, but I can measure it with an electrometer.

Casimir: Huh? I don't get it. Your rocks are just confusing!

Marie: Radiation is a kind of energy. And an electrometer is a tool. It measures something. That's enough school for today!

Joseph: Why don't you children go find Aunt Marie some special rocks. Then she can look at them to remember this time we had together.

Narrator 1: The two children run off toward a small stream that flows nearby. The adults continue to talk.

Narrator 2: Father, Joseph, and Hela share stories about life back home. Marie and Bronya describe their lives in Paris. Soon, the children come running back.

Lena: Aunt Marie, look what we've found!

Narrator 1: Lena holds out a rock. It is white and powdery to the touch.

Joseph: Hey! That's quite a rock! Marie, do you think this is a "special" rock?

Marie: I know this is a rock I can write with. Watch as I make a mark on this other rock. And of course it is special because Lena found it for me. It is a rock called chalk.

Father: What about you, Casimir? Did you find anything.

Casimir: Yes, I did. How is this for special?

Narrator 2: Casimir holds out his hand. In it, he has a milky rock with jagged edges.

Casimir: Aunt Marie, isn't this a piece of quartz?

Marie: Yes, it is.

Casimir: See, Aunt Marie isn't the only one who knows things about rocks in this family.

Joseph: [grinning] But we're not talking about the rocks in your head, you know.

Lena: Wait! I have one more. Look.

Narrator 1: Lena holds out another rock. This one is dull gray with bits of white embedded in it.

Discoverers and Inventors Reader's Theater © 2004 Creative Teaching Press

Bronya: That is a rock I recognize. It is a sedimentary rock. All those little white bits? Look really closely.

Lena: Oh! They're little shells!

Bronya: Those are fossils. The shells fell into the sediments at the bottom of the sea and were compressed until they became a part of a rock. I bet there are even little bits of bone in there.

Casimir: Hey! I can top that rock. I remember another rock I saw by the water's edge. I'll be right back.

Narrator 2: Casimir turns and runs back toward the trees at the edge of the stream. He searches around, finds what he was looking for, and runs back to the group.

Casimir: Ta da!

Joseph: [beginning to laugh] That's a topper all right.

Bronya: Oh, yuck. Casimir put that down.

Casimir: What? I think this is a pretty unique rock. It's more interesting than Lena's.

Marie: It's interesting, but it is not a rock. It's an owl pellet.

Casimir: Ewww! A what? Is an owl pellet what I think it is?

Hela: [laughing] I think I know what you're thinking, and it isn't that bad. An owl pellet is the bones and fur from a small animal an owl eats but can't digest. It spits it back up as this little ball.

Casimir: I'll be right back. It may not be as bad, but I still want to go wash my hands in the creek.

Joseph: It's a good thing no one has walked a dog here or ridden a horse by lately. Just imagine the kind of "rock" we could have seen then.

Marie: Yes, I think Casimir needs to spend a little more time studying rocks!

Discoverers and Inventors Reader's Theater © 2004 Creative Teaching Press

RELATED LESSONS

Researching the Elements

OBJECTIVE
Use research materials to find information.

ACTIVITY

Explain that Marie and Pierre Curie discovered the element radium. The symbol for radium is Ra and its atomic number is 88 on the periodic table. Provide **dictionaries, charts of the periodic table of elements,** or the **Internet** for students to use. Write on the board the list of elements shown below. Ask students to list the elements in alphabetical order and find the symbol and atomic weight for each element.

Hydrogen	Carbon	Radon	Silver
Helium	Nitrogen	Platinum	Calcium
Sodium	Potassium	Gold	Mercury
Iron	Phosphorus	Copper	Sulfur
Zinc	Lead	Oxygen	Neon

ANSWERS

Calcium, Ca, 20	Lead, Pb, 82	Potassium, K, 19
Carbon, C, 6	Mercury, Hg, 80	Radon, Rn, 86
Copper, Cu, 29	Neon, Ne, 10	Silver, Ag, 47
Gold, Au, 79	Nitrogen, N, 7	Sodium, Na, 11
Helium, He, 2	Oxygen, O, 8	Sulfur, S, 16
Hydrogen, H, 1	Phosphorus, P, 15	Zinc, Zn, 30
Iron, Fe, 26	Platinum, Pt, 78	

The Changing Face of Europe

OBJECTIVE
Familiarize students with how political boundaries on maps change over time.

ACTIVITY

Give each student a **Map of Europe, 1867 reproducible (page 68).** Explain to students that when Marie Curie was born, the map of European countries looked different than it does now. When Marie was a little girl, Poland was a part of the Russian Empire. Provide students with a **variety of maps and atlases of the European continent.** Ask students to research how Europe is divided into countries today. Have them use **colored pencils** to draw in the new country borders on their map. Have them create a key that names the countries that they added to their map.

Map of Europe, 1867

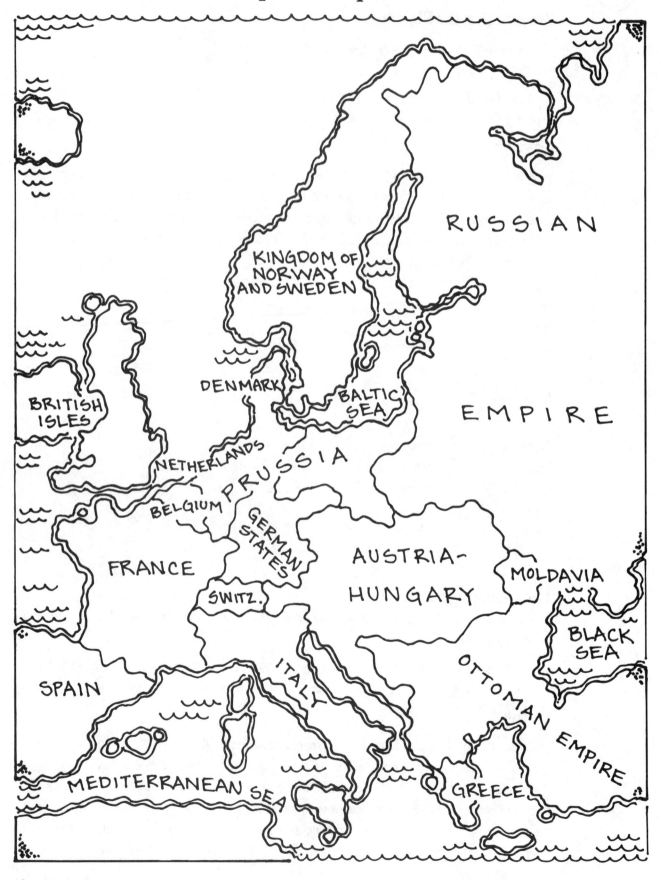

RUSSIAN

KINGDOM OF
NORWAY
AND SWEDEN

DENMARK

BALTIC
SEA

EMPIRE

BRITISH
ISLES

NETHERLANDS

PRUSSIA

BELGIUM

GERMAN
STATES

AUSTRIA-

FRANCE

SWITZ.

HUNGARY

MOLDAVIA

BLACK
SEA

SPAIN

ITALY

OTTOMAN EMPIRE

MEDITERRANEAN SEA

GREECE

Discoverers and Inventors Reader's Theater © 2004 Creative Teaching Press

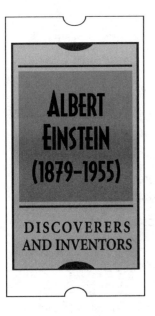

Vocabulary

Discuss each of the following words with students. Then, have students discuss how they could learn more about the meaning of each word.

converses: talks to

disheveled: marked by disorder or disarray

niceties: good manners

psychoanalysis: a study of the mind developed by Sigmund Freud where dreams, the subconscious, and repressed emotions are explored and analyzed

repressed: held back or controlled one's emotions

subconscious: part of the mind below the conscious, which is where one is aware of things

Background

As a child, Albert Einstein was so slow in his verbal abilities that his teachers didn't think he'd amount to much. Later, Albert did not respond well to the rote teaching style that was popular at the time, but he was brilliant in math and physics. After Einstein wrote his papers, including his theory of relativity, he was sought out as a lecturer and teacher. He met many other well-known people of his time, including Sigmund Freud. Albert and his wife, Elsa, fled Germany when Hitler came to power. Since he was a pacifist and Jewish, his life was in danger.

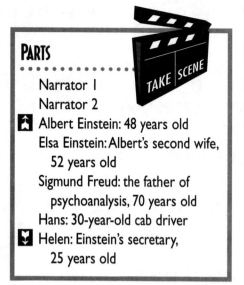

PARTS

Narrator 1
Narrator 2
Albert Einstein: 48 years old
Elsa Einstein: Albert's second wife,
  52 years old
Sigmund Freud: the father of
  psychoanalysis, 70 years old
Hans: 30-year-old cab driver
Helen: Einstein's secretary,
  25 years old

FLUENCY INSTRUCTION

Have students discuss the ages of the characters to help them reflect the maturity level in their reading. When you read aloud the script for students, have them listen for the following:

- All of the characters are adults. Have students note that when the group contains no children, the conversation is evenly paced and adults speak in lower tones.

- At one point, the cabdriver responds to Freud with an emphatic *Thank you, sir!* Ask students to explain what this reaction tells you about what is happening in the story.

- This line has a question mark at the end but is not phrased like a question: **Freud:** *I presume that you are Albert Einstein since I am assured this is the correct address?* Have students name other ways Freud could have asked this question such as *Are you Albert Einstein?* Invite students to explain how these different questions change the meaning or change the style in which the character speaks.

- Freud responds to Albert with a *Yessss.* Explain that by stretching out the word in this manner, it shows that Freud is considering what he has just been told. When a character is thinking, his or her speech slows down and the pause between words increases.

COMPREHENSION

After you read aloud the script, ask students these questions:

1. Who is Dr. Freud?

2. Why has Sigmund Freud come to call on Albert Einstein?

3. Compare Elsa to her husband. How is her manner different? How is it the same?

4. When Freud says that he finds the people of Berlin repressed, Albert responds that if they aren't now, they will be. What do you think Einstein means by this statement?

5. If you could ask Albert Einstein a question, and have him explain it in a way you would understand, what would your question be?

TELL ME ABOUT YOUR CHILDHOOD

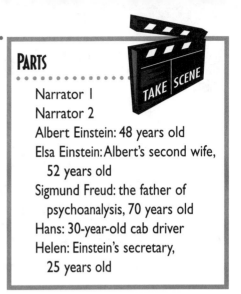

PARTS

Narrator 1
Narrator 2
Albert Einstein: 48 years old
Elsa Einstein: Albert's second wife,
   52 years old
Sigmund Freud: the father of
   psychoanalysis, 70 years old
Hans: 30-year-old cab driver
Helen: Einstein's secretary,
   25 years old

Narrator 1: In 1927, Doctor Sigmund Freud visits Germany. When Albert Einstein hears of this visit, he invites Freud to his home. Freud is as famous in the field of psychology as Einstein is in the field of physics.

Narrator 2: Albert Einstein enjoys discussing ideas with a variety of people. Although he most often converses with other physicists, he is excited to hold a discussion with the famous Dr. Freud.

Hans: Here you go, sir. This is the place you want.

Freud: This is the home of Albert Einstein and his wife?

Hans: Yes it is, sir.

Freud: Very well then. Here is my fare. I thank you for your service.

Hans: [appreciatively] Thank you, sir! Would you like me to wait? Or perhaps you would like me to call for you in an hour or so?

Freud: Good idea. Yes, call back in an hour. Surely I will be ready for a cab to the hotel.

Hans: Very good, sir.

Narrator 1: As Sigmund Freud walks up the steps and approaches, the door is suddenly flung open. In the doorway stands a man.

Narrator 2: He is smiling warmly and looks eager to greet the doctor, even though his clothes are disheveled and it looks as though he has not combed his hair in days.

Albert: Dr. Freud! It is so good to meet you, so good for you to come. Come in, come in. ELSA! Our company has arrived.

Freud: I presume that you are Albert Einstein since I am assured this is the correct address?

Albert: Oh, yes, yes. That is I. I am Albert Einstein. I apologize for my lapse in good manners. I have a lot going on in my head and sometimes I forget about the niceties.

Freud: Hmmm, I see. That is interesting. Perhaps when you were a child something happened to make you this way?

Albert: What? As a child? Uh, no. I don't think so. My brain is very busy with thoughts of physics. It makes me preoccupied is all.

Freud: Hmmm, very interesting.

Elsa: Good day to you, Herr Freud. Welcome to our home. Please, come in.

Freud: I see that your wife has experienced no childhood trauma to affect her manners.

Elsa: I beg your pardon?

Albert: [to Elsa] Never mind. He seems to think my absentmindedness started in my childhood.

Elsa: That wouldn't surprise me in the least. You've been absentminded since I have known you.

Freud: Hmmm, interesting. What a lovely collection of photographs. Are they all family?

Elsa: Why, thank you. Yes, most of them are. My family and Albert's as well. Although we share some family members since we are cousins.

Freud: You are cousins? That is interesting.

Albert: You keep saying that. Why is that interesting?

Freud: Everything about a person is interesting in psychoanalysis. Tell me, do you have any dreams?

Elsa: Dreams? What a strange thing to ask. What is so interesting about dreams?

Albert: Dr. Freud thinks that dreams are the way our subconscious tries to tell us things, Elsa.

Elsa: Oh. I can't remember my dreams anyway.

Freud: Really? Hmmm, that is interesting.

Narrator 1: Helen, Albert's secretary, brings in a large silver tray filled with a teapot, cups, sugar, cream, and teacakes.

Discoverers and Inventors Reader's Theater © 2004 Creative Teaching Press

TELL ME ABOUT YOUR CHILDHOOD

Narrator 2: She looks about nervously. Helen has never quite gotten used to the idea that she works with such a famous man as Albert Einstein. Now here is another famous man, Sigmund Freud.

Elsa: Dr. Freud, this is my husband's secretary, Helen Dukas. Helen, this is Doctor Freud.

Helen: I am very pleased to meet you, sir.

Freud: Interesting. Why do you say that?

Helen: What? I don't, um, understand.

Albert: [sarcastically] You hear that, Freud? Perhaps it is something in her childhood.

Freud: Yessss. Perhaps it is. Tell me, Helen, can you remember what you dreamed about last night?

Narrator 1: Helen's face suddenly turns bright red. She is nervous enough and she doesn't understand why this important man is asking about her dreams.

Helen: I, uh, don't, um, well, it's just that . . .

Elsa: It's okay, Helen. Thank you for the tea. We'll let you know if we need anything else.

Helen: [with great relief] You're welcome, Elsa. I will be upstairs if you need me.

Freud: Hmmm, interesting.

Albert: Why do you keep saying that?!

Freud: Saying what?

Albert: That everything is so interesting! How can *anything* be interesting when *everything* is interesting?!

Freud: It's interesting that you feel that way, Albert.

Albert: Agggghhhhh!

Elsa: So tell us, Doctor Freud, have you enjoyed your stay here in Berlin?

Freud: Yes, I find it . . .

Albert: [exasperated] Interesting??

Freud: Actually, I would say stimulating. I find that people seem rather repressed.

Discoverers and Inventors Reader's Theater © 2004 Creative Teaching Press

Albert: [muttering] If they aren't now, they soon will be.

Freud: What was that, Albert?

Albert: Oh, nothing. Just talking to myself.

Freud: Hmmm, interesting. So, Albert, tell me, this theory of relativity of yours. What does it mean?

Narrator 2: This is a question Albert can answer. He wants nothing more than to help people understand his work.

Narrator 1: As Albert warms to his subject, he gets more and more excited. As he goes, he talks at a more and more rapid pace.

Albert: The basic idea is that the speed of anything is relative to the position of other objects and their speed.

Elsa: Use the bus example, dear. It helps.

Albert: Oh, okay. Say a man is on a bus and he is walking toward the front of the bus. He is traveling at, say, two miles per hour. But the bus is traveling at ten miles per hour. To the people on the bus, the man is moving at two miles per hour. But say you are watching from the street. The man would be moving at his speed plus the speed of the bus. The passenger's speed is relative to where you are.

Elsa: Very good, dear.

Freud: Yes, I see. That *is* interesting.

Albert: And then if you were in outer space watching the man on the bus through a telescope, then not only is the speed of the man and the bus combined, but you have to take into account the speed at which the earth is rotating *and* the speed the earth is orbiting the sun!

Freud: That man would *really* be moving!

Albert: Exactly! It's all relative!

Narrator 1: Suddenly, there is a beeping of a horn outside on the street.

Freud: Has it been an hour already? That would be my cab.

Elsa: Must you go so soon, Doctor Freud?

Discoverers and Inventors Reader's Theater © 2004 Creative Teaching Press

Freud:	It will be suppertime soon. I will leave you to your evening, Mrs. Einstein.
Albert:	[to himself] But of course, if it were light instead of the man, then the position of the earth in relation to the sun …
Freud:	Is Albert okay?
Elsa:	Oh, absolutely. He gets like this. Once he gets to thinking about his theories and his physics, it's as though he is alone in the room.
Freud:	Good day to you, Mrs. Einstein. Good day, Albert!
Albert:	What? Who? Oh, yes, good day, uh, yes, good day.
Narrator 1:	Elsa shows Sigmund Freud to the door and waves good-bye as he enters the cab. She shuts the door behind her.
Freud:	Thank you for returning.
Hans:	And how was your meeting with the famous Albert Einstein?
Freud:	It was very interesting. He is an unusual little man. I wonder what he was like as a child.
Hans:	That I wouldn't know. Didn't know him as a child. But he sure is a smart man.
Freud:	So I hear. However, I came to realize that Einstein knows as much about psychology as I know about physics. But never mind. So, my dear sir, tell me about your mother …

RELATED LESSONS

Einstein's Circle of Friends

OBJECTIVE

Identify and research some of Einstein's contemporaries.

ACTIVITY

Explain that as Albert Einstein became more well-known, other famous scientists and politicians sought him out. Provide students with research materials such as **books and/or the Internet.** Have them choose one of the people listed below. Ask students to find out where this individual lived, for what he or she is well-known, and his or her relationship to Einstein. Have students take notes. Invite them to share their findings with the class.

Pablo Picasso	Sigmund Freud	Marie Curie
Adolf Hitler	Jakob Einstein	Caesar Koch
Max Planck	Mohandas Gandhi	Warren G. Harding
Edwin Hubble	Winston Churchill	Franklin D. Roosevelt

Moving About

OBJECTIVE

Plot locations and track a course on a map.

ACTIVITY

Give each student an **Einstein's Life Journey reproducible (page 77)** and a **highlighter.** Explain that Albert Einstein lived in many countries during his lifetime. Ask students to read the paragraph at the bottom of the page and highlight each of the locations where Einstein lived. Provide students with a **globe or an atlas.** Have them find each of the highlighted locations on the globe or in an atlas and mark that location on their reproducible. Ask students to write the date of Einstein's arrival next to each location. Then, have students draw lines with arrows to show the direction of Einstein's travel. Invite students to compare their maps.

Name_____ Date _____

Einstein's Life Journey

Directions: Read the passage below and highlight the locations that tell where Albert Einstein lived. Find and mark each location on the map. Write the date next to the location. Draw arrows to show the direction of Einstein's moves.

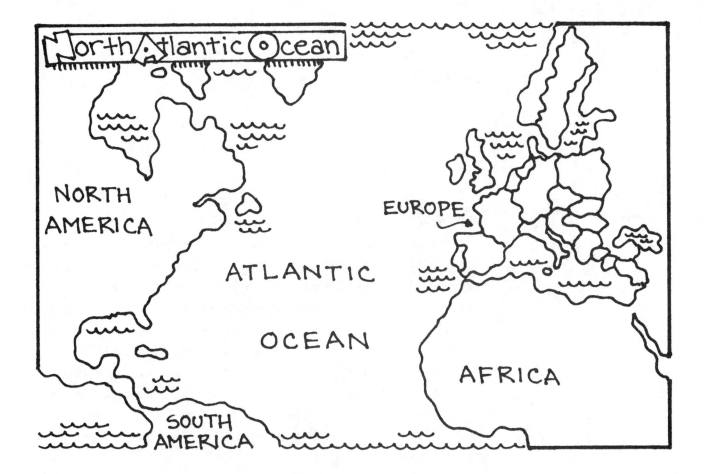

Albert Einstein was born in Ulm, Germany, on March 14, 1879. In 1880, the Einstein family moved to Munich, Germany, and lived there until 1894. At that time, Albert's father's business was doing poorly and the family decided to move to Milan, Italy, for better opportunities. At first, Albert remained behind to finish school, but in 1895 he also left Germany and joined his family in Italy. In 1896, Albert was accepted into college in Zurich, Switzerland. Albert accepted a full-time position at the University of Prague in the Czech Republic in 1911. In 1914, Albert now had a family of his own, and they all moved to Berlin, Germany. In 1933, Albert Einstein and his family settled in Princeton, New Jersey, to escape growing tensions in Germany prior to World War II.

Discoverers and Inventors Reader's Theater © 2004 Creative Teaching Press

RACHEL CARSON (1907–1964)

DISCOVERERS AND INVENTORS

VOCABULARY

Discuss each of the following words with students. Then, have students sort the words by parts of speech.

bedroll: a roll of bedding carried by a traveler (n)

engulf: swallow something up (v)

liable: responsible for, by law (adj)

privilege: a special right given to a person or group (n)

solitude: state of being alone (n)

suffragette: a woman campaigning for the right to vote (n)

BACKGROUND

When she was 55 years old, Rachel Carson's book *Silent Spring* was published, and the world began to realize the effects of our chemical use on the environment. However, Rachel's interest in nature began long before that. As the youngest child in a family of five, she was encouraged by her suffragette mother to think for herself. Rachel always had a love for the sea and read everything she could find about it as a child. Her studies in college centered around biology, but it wasn't until the summer of 1929 when she actually saw the sea for the first time. In this imaginary dialogue, a much younger Rachel and her family take a trip to the ocean, and already her concern about the environment is apparent. In reality, her family members were probably just as concerned about the environment as she was.

PARTS

Narrator 1
Narrator 2
Rachel: 7 years old
Robert (Junior): Rachel's
  15-year-old brother
Marian: Rachel's 17-year-old sister
Mom (Maria Carson):
  Rachel's mother
Dad (Robert Carson):
  Rachel's father

FLUENCY INSTRUCTION

Have students discuss the ages of the characters to help them reflect the maturity level in their reading. When you read aloud the script for students, have them listen for the following:

• There is an 8-year age difference between Rachel and her brother and sister. Have students discuss how a teenager talks to a younger child and teenagers talk to each other.

• Marian does not find her encounter with nature a pleasant one. Your voice gets louder and certain words are stressed to show panic as Marian encounters the sea anemone and the snake.

• Some of the words are written in all capital letters. Your voice becomes loud and shrill when you read words in all capital letters.

COMPREHENSION

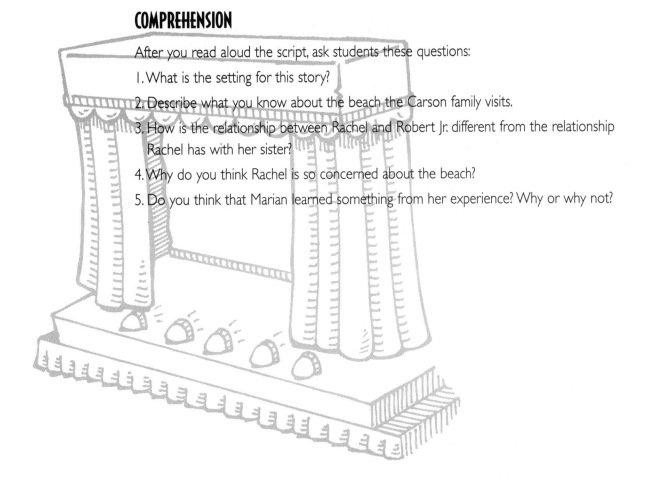

After you read aloud the script, ask students these questions:

1. What is the setting for this story?

2. Describe what you know about the beach the Carson family visits.

3. How is the relationship between Rachel and Robert Jr. different from the relationship Rachel has with her sister?

4. Why do you think Rachel is so concerned about the beach?

5. Do you think that Marian learned something from her experience? Why or why not?

A Day at the Beach

PARTS

Narrator 1
Narrator 2
Rachel: 7 years old
Robert (Junior): Rachel's
    15-year-old brother
Marian: Rachel's 17-year-old sister
Mom (Maria Carson):
    Rachel's mother
Dad (Robert Carson):
    Rachel's father

Narrator 1: Waves crash on the rocks and sand and roll back into the roiling surf. A slight breeze blows the sea grasses. Gulls cry overhead.

Narrator 2: The sky is clear and sunny. In the distance are two small canvas tents. A man and a woman are bent over a campfire. The smell of fresh coffee is strong in the air.

Narrator 1: One tent is empty because Robert and Maria Carson are already up and preparing for breakfast. For a moment, the adults enjoy the solitude of this lovely morning.

Narrator 2: But sounds can be heard from the second tent. They know their peace and quiet is about to come to an end. They look at each other and sigh.

Mom: Good morning, sleepyhead. Did you sleep okay last night?

Rachel: The waves put me to sleep. I slept great, except Marian kept hogging all the room in the tent.

Marian: That's the privilege when you are the oldest.

Rachel: And the biggest. [to her mother] Isn't it beautiful, Mother? It is everything I pictured it to be. I can't wait to explore.

Dad: First you need some breakfast. Is your brother up?

Robert: Yeah, I'm up.

Narrator 1: Nothing tastes quite as good as a breakfast cooked on a campfire first thing in the morning.

Narrator 2: There is very little discussion between any of the Carson family members as they wolf down their eggs, bacon, and fresh coffee.

Dad: I want all of you to stick together this morning.

Robert: Aw, Dad! Why?

Discoverers and Inventors Reader's Theater © 2004 Creative Teaching Press

Dad:	Especially with Rachel. I don't want her wandering off by herself.
Mom:	I don't think Rachel is the one we need to worry about. She has more common sense than all of us put together.
Rachel:	[beaming] Don't worry, Dad. I'll keep an eye on Robert so he won't get into trouble.
Robert:	And we'll both keep an eye on Marian, especially if there are any boys around. She's liable to fall into the ocean and not know it.
Marian:	Oh, Robert. Grow up.
Mom:	Regardless, I do want to know where you are going. I don't want any of you wandering off too far.
Narrator 1:	Rachel grabs her notebook and pencil and starts off down the beach toward the rocks.
Narrator 2:	Robert begins to follow her. He knows he'll have a busy day keeping up with Rachel.
Marian:	Wait a second, Robert. Let me fix my hair.
Robert:	Wait a second?! I didn't know you had speeded things up lately. Seems to me it will take you a lot longer than a second. Rachel's heading to the rocks. Catch up with us there.
Rachel:	Robert! Come see!
Robert:	What is it? Oh, wow! It's like a little ocean all by itself.
Rachel:	I've read about this. It's a tide pool. When the tide is high, water covers the rocks here and fills the holes up with water. When the tide is low, this water stays behind. Look at all the animals that live here!
Marian:	I don't see any animals. It looks like a bunch of plants and rocks to me.
Rachel:	Oh, hello, Marian. I did not think you would be here so soon. This is seaweed and it is a plant, but this thing here is neither a plant nor a rock. It's a sea anemone.
Robert:	A what?
Rachel:	A sea anemone. It attaches itself to the rocks and dangles its tentacles. Then, when something tasty swims too close, the anemone stings it with its tentacles and wraps itself around the food to eat it.
Marian:	How do you know that?
Rachel:	I read it in a book.

A Day at the Beach

Robert: She reads things, Marian. You might want to try it sometime.

Marian: I'm ignoring you, Robert.

Rachel: Oh, look! Watch what happens.

Narrator 1: As the three watch, a small shrimp ventures too close to the waving tentacles of the anemone. All of a sudden, the tentacles wrap around the shrimp and engulf it.

Robert: Whoa! Did you see that? It looks like it turned itself inside out!

Marian: Ewww! Gross! Why did it do that?

Rachel: That's how it hunts for food. Hey! Don't throw rocks at it!

Marian: You are weird, Rachel. Do what you want. I'll be over here.

Robert: Just ignore her, Rach. She's not interested in this stuff.

Rachel: But she should be. They are living things too, just like us. We share this planet with all of these living things.

Robert: I know that, but Marian doesn't appreciate nature the way you do. You make a good teacher, Rachel. Maybe you can teach her.

Rachel: I don't know. She thinks I'm too little. I don't think she'll listen to what I say.

Robert: Maybe in some way you can teach her to care.

Narrator 2: Suddenly, Robert and Rachel hear Marian cry out. From behind a tuft of sea grass, they can see Marian swinging a stick at some unknown foe on the ground. The children run up to her.

Robert: What's wrong, Marian? Are you all right?

Marian: Yuck! It was a snake. It just snuck up on me. I hate snakes.

Rachel: Oh, Marian. Look what you've done! You have torn up the sand and the grass here with that stick. Don't you know this is the snake's home? You scared it more than it scared you.

Marian: I doubt that. I don't like surprises like that.

Rachel: Stop with the stick, Marian. How would you like it if an animal came into your home and started stirring it up with a stick.

Discoverers and Inventors Reader's Theater © 2004 Creative Teaching Press

Marian: Don't be silly, Rachel. That's not likely to happen, now is it?

Narrator 1: Marian starts back to the tents. Robert and Rachel continue to explore the tide pools and sea grasses. Every once in a while, Rachel stops and draws intently in her notebook.

Narrator 2: Later in the day, the family finishes a noontime meal.

Dad: Rachel, come with me and help me collect some driftwood for the fire. We need to boil some water before your mother can clean the dishes.

Mom: Robert, Marian, would you help me clean things up? The food needs to be put away and I could use some help collecting the dishes.

Dad: Thanks for your help, Rachel. And that's quite an education you gave me about the bird we saw. I'm impressed by how much you know.

Rachel: I just read a lot, that's all. Hey, Mom, what is Marian doing?

Mom: I don't know. She was helping us clean up.

Robert: Last I saw she had all the empty bottles and cans from lunch.

Narrator 1: Rachel runs up to her sister to find Marian is attempting to bury some containers and paper wrappers in a hole in the sand.

Rachel: You can't do that, Marian!

Marian: I have to put it somewhere, silly. We can't keep a bunch of garbage in our tent!

Rachel: But you are just putting it in someone else's home! You can't bury it here on the beach. Do you think the animals want this garbage where they live?

Marian: How do you know the animals even care, Rachel? Don't tell me you have started talking to them now.

Rachel: No. But it is so beautiful here. I don't want you messing it up. If everyone left their garbage here, imagine what it would look like.

Marian: Rachel, you are too young. When you are older, you'll understand how the world works. Everything can't be the way you want it, you know.

Narrator 2: Rachel gives up arguing with her sister. She just doesn't know how to make Marian understand what is so important to her.

Narrator 1: But as she heads back to her family, an idea comes to her. Rachel runs down the beach, collecting bits of rock, sand, and grass.

A Day at the Beach

Narrator 2:   Later that evening, the family prepares for bed.

Marian: AHHH! What is all this stuff on my bed roll?!

Dad: What is wrong with you, Marian?

Marian: Look at my bed, Dad. It's covered with rocks, sand, sticks, and grass! Why is all of this here? RACHEL!!

Rachel: I wanted you to see what it felt like to have someone dump their garbage into your home.

Robert: [laughing] You have an interesting way of proving your point, Rach.

Marian: MOM, make her clean it up!

Mom: Marian, maybe Rachel has a point. You know these things are important to her. But, Rachel, I think you've taught Marian enough for one day. Help your sister clean up this mess.

Robert: Oh, I don't know. Marian may need a few more lessons like this.

Dad: That's enough, Robert.

Mom: Get to it, girls. Get this cleaned up. It's time for bed.

Dad: You have to admit, Maria. Our family vacations are never dull.

Discoverers and Inventors Reader's Theater © 2004 Creative Teaching Press

RELATED LESSONS

Tide Pool Diagrams

OBJECTIVE
Identify the living and nonliving characteristics of a tide pool.

ACTIVITY

Explain that when Rachel Carson was a young girl, she was fascinated by the ocean even though she had never been there. Have students make a diagram of a tide pool. Provide research materials such as **books or the Internet.** Ask students to find out what plants and animals interact in a tide pool. Have students find out how the tide affects different levels of the tide pool. Then, ask students to draw a cross section of a tide pool and label the various parts. Have students share and explain their diagrams with the class.

Birds of North America

OBJECTIVE
Read a data sheet to find information.

ACTIVITY

Give each student a **Birds of North America reproducible (page 86).** Have students look over the reproducible and note the type of information listed. Invite them to take turns asking questions such as *Which bird is 10½ inches in length?* Divide the class into small groups. Have each group use the information on the reproducible to make a graph that compares one fact about all the birds. Have groups share the completed graphs with the class.

Birds of North America

Mourning Dove
length: 10¹/₂ inches (27 cm)
wingspan: 13 inches (33 cm)
nests on 2 eggs

Pileated Woodpecker
length: 15 inches (38 cm)
wingspan: 21 inches (53 cm)
nests on up to 8 eggs

Barn Owl
length: 14 inches (36 cm)
wingspan: 44 inches (110 cm)
nests on up to 8 eggs

Arctic Tern
length: 15 inches (38 cm)
wingspan: 31 inches (77.5 cm)
nests on up to 4 eggs

Canvasback Duck
length: 13 inches (33 cm)
wingspan: 31 inches (77.5 cm)
nests on up to 14 eggs

Wood Ibis
length: 35 inches (87.5 cm)
wingspan: 3¹/₂ feet (1.01 m)
nests on up to 6 eggs

Peregrine Falcon
length: 15 inches (38 cm)
wingspan: 40 inches (100 cm)
nests on up to 6 eggs

Ivory Gull
length: 14 inches (36 cm)
wingspan: 41 inches (102.5 cm)
nests on up to 5 eggs

Flamingo
length: 42 inches (105 cm)
wingspan: 55 inches (137.5 cm)
nests on up to 6 eggs

JANE GOODALL (1934–)

DISCOVERERS AND INVENTORS

VOCABULARY

Discuss each of the following words with students. Then, have students identify the word they least understand. Have students research this word and then draw an illustration that clarifies the definition.

avoid: to act in a way that prevents contact

famished: very hungry

Mum: slang for Mom

BACKGROUND

Because of World War II, Jane Goodall and her family moved to the countryside of England. Here she was able to explore the neighboring farmland. Her interest in animal behavior began when she was very young. She wanted to see how a chicken laid an egg and she hid inside a henhouse to find out, although her sister was never a witness to that event. The book *The Story of Doctor Doolittle* also inspired her to seek out more information about animal behavior. It is her work with chimpanzees, and her tireless efforts to protect them, for which she is most famous.

PARTS

Narrator 1
Narrator 2
Jane Goodall: 7 years old
Margaret: Jane's mother
Mortimer: Jane's father
Judy: Jane's younger sister,
   5 years old
Nanny: the girls' caretaker,
   16 years old
Uncle Rex: Jane's uncle and her
   father's brother

FLUENCY INSTRUCTION

Have students discuss the ages of the characters to help them reflect the maturity level in their reading. When you read aloud the script for students, have them listen for the following:

• The pace of the reading speeds up when the children are excited, such as when they both realize the hen has laid an egg. Have students listen to distinguish between Jane's excitement and Judy's panic about the event.

• The volume decreases when the children are hiding in a small space. Have students name at least one place where the characters talk in a whisper. Model for students a "stage whisper." Point out that the characters cannot really whisper or the audience will not hear them.

• Nanny is a caretaker and therefore an employee of the family. Have students notice that Nanny is somewhat proper in her speech and manner toward the rest of the family.

COMPREHENSION

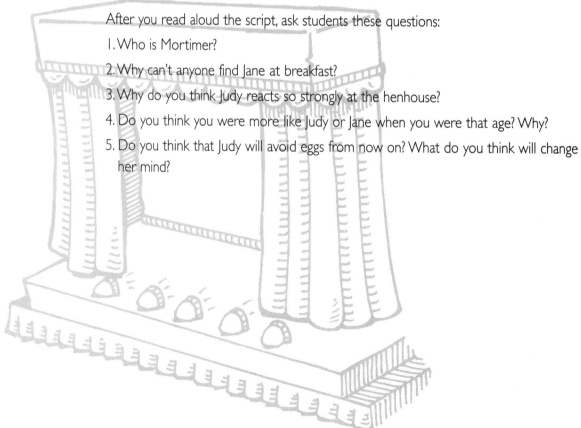

After you read aloud the script, ask students these questions:

1. Who is Mortimer?

2. Why can't anyone find Jane at breakfast?

3. Why do you think Judy reacts so strongly at the henhouse?

4. Do you think you were more like Judy or Jane when you were that age? Why?

5. Do you think that Judy will avoid eggs from now on? What do you think will change her mind?

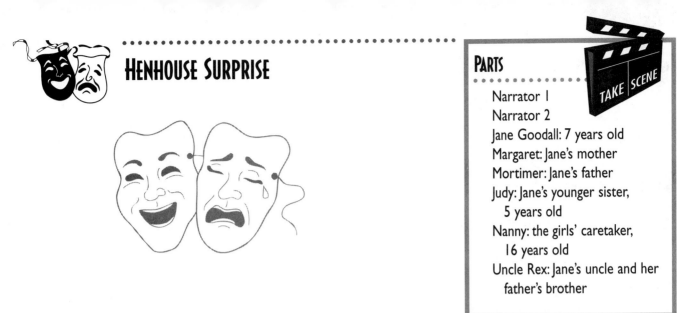

Henhouse Surprise

Parts

Narrator 1
Narrator 2
Jane Goodall: 7 years old
Margaret: Jane's mother
Mortimer: Jane's father
Judy: Jane's younger sister,
   5 years old
Nanny: the girls' caretaker,
   16 years old
Uncle Rex: Jane's uncle and her
   father's brother

Narrator 1: During World War II, Jane Goodall's family moved to the safety of the countryside in England.

Narrator 2: Jane often liked to wake earlier than the others and go off to find and watch the animals on the farm. That is exactly what has happened this fine spring morning.

Mortimer: Good morning, everyone. Something smells good. Is Jane still sleeping?

Margaret: Usually Jane is the first one up. Judy, is your sister still in her room?

Judy: I don't think so. If she is, she's being awfully quiet.

Uncle Rex: That doesn't sound like Jane.

Nanny: She isn't in her room. I checked before I came down here.

Judy: Do you want me to get her, Mum?

Margaret: No. Eat your breakfast. She'll be famished and be here any minute.

Narrator 1: The family continues with breakfast.

Narrator 2: Even after the dishes are cleared, Jane is nowhere to be found.

Nanny: Ma'am, would you like me to go see where Jane has gone off to?

Mortimer: I wouldn't worry much. You know how Jane is.

Judy: She's probably avoiding us so she doesn't have to do any schoolwork.

Nanny: Jane likes her schoolwork. She wouldn't hide from that.

Uncle Rex: She didn't have any exams today, did she? Any work to turn in, Nanny?

Nanny: No, nothing at all.

HENHOUSE SURPRISE

Margaret:	She has to be around here somewhere. It's such a lovely day. She must be outside already.
Mortimer:	Not like her to pass up a meal though. Judy, go look about for your sister.
Nanny:	Put on your shoes first!
Judy:	All right. I'll find her.
Narrator 1:	Jane is indeed outside, at least outside the house anyway. She is inside the barn and has been there for the last half hour.
Narrator 2:	Jane is naturally curious about everything, but especially curious about animals. She watches animals all the time.
Narrator 1:	And on this particular morning, she has been watching the chickens. She became very curious when one of the hens headed into the henhouse.
Narrator 2:	The henhouse is a lean-to structure against the outside of one side of the barn. Jane can see into the henhouse through a large hole in the barn wall.
Jane:	[very softly] That's okay, Miss Chickie. I will be very quiet as I keep you company. You just go about your business.
Judy:	Jane! What are you doing?
Jane:	Shhhhhh! You'll scare her.
Judy:	[quietly] Sorry! Scare who? Is someone else here?
Jane:	Just Miss Chickie. In the henhouse. She's on her nest.
Judy:	Why is she on her nest? It's daytime. Shouldn't she be outside pecking for worms or something?
Jane:	Just watch and see what happens. I noticed she came in here a bit ago. I discovered I could watch the hens from this hole in the wall here. What do you see?
Judy:	She's just sitting there.
Jane:	No, really. What do you see? Look closely. What does she do from moment to moment?
Judy:	Well . . . she kind of rocks back and forth. And she's clucking, isn't she? Kind of like she's talking to herself.
Jane:	Yes, sort of. That's what I noticed, too.

Discoverers and Inventors Reader's Theater © 2004 Creative Teaching Press

Henhouse Surprise

Narrator 1: As the two girls watch, the hen continues to cluck softly.

Narrator 2: Then, the hen changed her position slightly.

Judy: Is she getting up?

Jane: I don't think so. Keep watching. I think I know what will happen next.

Judy: She doesn't seem to be able to make up her mind.

Narrator 1: Then, suddenly the hen raises herself forward a little . . .

Narrator 2: And an egg slides out of her body. Plop! Just like that.

Judy: [loudly] Aghhhh! What happened? What's wrong with her?

Narrator 1: The startled hen gives a loud squawk and bolts from the henhouse, flapping her wings.

Jane: Oh, Judy. Now you have scared her off.

Judy: But Jane, what happened to her? It's like she exploded.

Jane: She did not, you silly. She laid an egg.

Judy: Laid an egg?! That's where eggs come from? That's yucky!

Jane: Where did you think they came from? Did you think they just appeared in the nest each day?

Judy: I don't know. I never thought about it before. I just knew Mum got them from the henhouse. I'm never eating eggs again.

Jane: That's silly. You've eaten eggs before now.

Uncle Rex: There you are, Jane. We've been looking all over for you. [outside] Hello, everyone. They are in here, in the barn.

Judy: Oh, Uncle Rex, it was awful. The chicken pooped an egg!

Jane: No, she didn't! She laid one.

Uncle Rex: Judy, the hen didn't, um, have an egg that way. Eggs come from a different place.

Jane: Kind of like how you put eggs in your mouth, not in your nose. But they are both holes in your face!

Uncle Rex: Okay, I don't think I want to have this conversation anymore.

Henhouse Surprise

Mortimer: There you are! What on earth are you doing in here?

Margaret: Jane! I was getting a bit worried. I don't like it when you sneak off like that.

Uncle Rex: Apparently, Judy walked in on one of Janie's animal observations.

Judy: It was very weird, Papa. I thought the chicken exploded an egg, but Jane says it laid one. I don't like eggs anymore.

Margaret: Don't be silly, Judy. Of course you still like eggs. Jane, I think your sister is a bit too young to be a witness to such a thing.

Mortimer: She'll have nightmares.

Jane: About a chicken laying an egg?!

Nanny: Perhaps I should take the girls inside, ma'am?

Jane: I don't want to go inside yet. I want to watch the animals. It was so interesting. I never knew for sure how the hens laid an egg before now. She does this whole little dance to get the nest just right. You should have seen it.

Judy: I wish anyone would have seen it but me!

Uncle Rex: It's all part of living on a farm, Judy.

Mortimer: If we don't gather the eggs, the hens sit on them for a time. And then the eggs hatch into chicks.

Judy: What??!!!

Margaret: Mortimer, I don't think you're helping the situation much.

Uncle Rex: Hey, Jane. Have you been watching the new foal much? She is starting to act just like her mother.

Jane: No, I haven't. Can I go with Uncle Rex and see the foal? Just for a while? I promise I'll study harder this afternoon.

Nanny: I can go with her, ma'am. Just to make sure she stays out of trouble.

Margaret: Oh, all right. Thank you, Nanny. Come along, Judy. You can help me bake a cake for supper. I think we've learned enough for one day.

Judy: It doesn't have any eggs, does it?

Discoverers and Inventors Reader's Theater © 2004 Creative Teaching Press

RELATED LESSONS

Comparing the Apes

OBJECTIVE

Research and compare the four types of apes: gorilla, chimpanzee, orangutan, and gibbon.

ACTIVITY

Give each student a **Comparing the Apes reproducible (page 94).** Explain that the apes are the closest relative to humans in the animal world. Apes are different than monkeys in that they have no external tail and have more complex brains. Provide students with **research materials such as books and/or the Internet.** Have students work in small groups to research the facts on the reproducible. Ask them to write each fact in the appropriate column. Remind students that some of the facts will appear in more than one column. Encourage them to add any additional information they find. Invite groups to share their findings with the class.

ANSWERS

Gibbons	Orangutans	Gorillas	Chimpanzees
• have no tails • are mammals • sometimes eat meat • live in family units • slender, long-limbed animals • found only in the dense forests of Borneo and Sumatra	• found only in the tropical forests of Southeast Asia • have no tails • are mammals • large, heavy-bodied with reddish-orange hair • sometimes eat meat	• have no tails • are mammals • eat only plants • can weigh as much as 600 pounds (272 kg) • black-haired • live in family units • found in the tropical forests of Africa	• have no tails • are mammals • use simple tools • sometimes eat meat • make nests of branches on ground for sleeping • black-haired • probably most intelligent of the apes • live in family units • found in the tropical forests of Africa

Jane Goodall

OBJECTIVE

Learn more about Jane Goodall.

ACTIVITY

Give each student a **Jane Goodall reproducible (page 95)** and a **Jane Goodall Revisited reproducible (page 96).** Review the questions to set a purpose for the reading. Have students read the information about Jane Goodall and answer the questions. Discuss the answers as a class.

ANSWERS

1. Jane Goodall was born in London, England, in 1934.

2. She was able to explore the neighboring farmland.

3. *Have students subtract her birth year from the current year.*

4. She observed their use of tools and the way they communicated.

5. She was inspired to learn more about animal behavior.

6. She is best remembered for her work to establish animal sanctuaries.

Comparing the Apes

Directions: Use your research to write each fact in the correct column. Some statements may be written in more than one column.

Gibbons	Orangutans	Gorillas	Chimpanzees

- found only in the tropical forests of Southeast Asia
- found in the tropical forests of Africa
- found only in the dense forests of Borneo and Sumatra
- have no tails
- are mammals
- large, heavy-bodied with reddish-orange hair
- slender, long-limbed animals
- live in family units
- use simple tools
- eat only plants
- sometimes eat meat
- make nests of branches on ground for sleeping
- can weigh as much as 600 pounds (272 kg)
- black-haired
- probably most intelligent of the apes

Name_____ Date _____

Jane Goodall

Directions: Read the story and answer the questions on the next page.

Jane Goodall was born in London, England, in 1934. With the beginning of World War II, her family moved to the countryside of England. Here she was able to explore the neighboring farmland. Her interest in animal behavior began when she was very young. Jane spent a lot of time observing the farm animals. She watched how the animals interacted within their own species and with their human caretakers. She even wanted to see how a chicken laid an egg and she hid inside a henhouse to find out. After Jane read the book *The Story of Doctor Doolittle*, she was inspired to seek out more information about animal behavior. In the book, a veterinarian is able to communicate with various animals in a verbal language. The idea of communicating with animals intrigued Jane. As an adult, she began to study the behavior of chimpanzees in the wild. She observed the behavior patterns of chimpanzees. She watched them use bits of straw to pull ants out of an anthill and care for their young. Over time, the chimpanzees grew used to Jane's presence. They began to communicate with her, not by words, but with their actions. Jane worked tirelessly to protect the chimpanzees and set up sanctuaries in the wild. It is for these efforts that Jane Goodall is most famous. Today, Jane travels the world, lecturing about her work and raising money for continued research.

Discoverers and Inventors Reader's Theater © 2004 Creative Teaching Press

Jane Goodall Revisited

Directions: Read the passage about Jane Goodall and answer the questions.

1. Where and when was Jane Goodall born?

2. What was important about the family's move to the country?

3. How old is Jane today?

4. Name two things Jane observed about the chimpanzees.

5. What effect did reading *The Story of Dr. Doolittle* have on Jane?

6. For what is Jane Goodall best remembered?

Discoverers and Inventors Reader's Theater © 2004 Creative Teaching Press